"In the Name of Allāh, the Most Beneficent,
the Most Merciful"

Contents

Preface

In the name of Allāh ﷻ, we praise Him, seek His help and ask for His forgiveness. Whosoever Allāh ﷻ guides, none can misguide, and whomsoever He allows to fall astray, none can guide them. We bear witness that there is no one worthy of worship but Allāh ﷻ alone, and we bear witness that Muhammad ﷺ is His slave and the seal of His Messengers ﷺ. May peace, salutations and blessings be upon our guide, mentor, our final and beloved Prophet Muhammad ﷺ, upon his noble Sahābahs ؓ, Tābi'īn ؓ and upon those who follow their great lifestyles until the Day of Judgement.

This book "A Clear Victory" is an enlightening commentary of Sūrah Al-Fath. It is cited in Sahīh Al-Bukhāri regarding the virtue of this Sūrah that Sayyidunā Umar Ibn Al-Khattāb ؓ reported that the Messenger of Allāh ﷺ said: "This night a Sūrah was sent down to me that is more beloved to me than all what the sun shines over," then he read,

$$ إِنَّا فَتَحْنَا لَكَ فَتْحًا مُّبِينًا $$

"We have indeed accorded a triumph to you, a manifest triumph, indeed". (Sahīh Al-Bukhāri)

In this beautiful Sūrah, six themes have been mentioned.

1. The treaty of Hudaybiyah and its consequences (48:1-7)
2. Tasks of Prophet Muhammad ﷺ (48:8-10)
3. The conditions of those who lagged from the treaty of Al-Hudaybiyah (48:11-17)

4. Bay'at Ar-Ridwān and its significance (48:18-24)
5. Reasons and influences of the treaty of Al-Hudaybiyah (48:25-26)
6. The Prophet's ﷺ vision comes true i.e. the conquest of Makkah Mukarramah (48:27-29)

There is a lot to learn and discover from this Sūrah. Nevertheless, the most comprehensive lesson is to ponder over an incredible emphasis on peace, dialogue, reconciliation and harmony in Islām as opposed to an armed struggle and war, even if defensive.

May Allāh ﷻ grant us all the ability to contemplate on the noble verses of the Qur'ān and give us the ability to act on the virtuous messages it conveys and may it illuminate our hearts. May Allāh ﷻ accept the efforts of all those participating in the writing and compilation of this book.

I would like to express my sincere gratitude to my respected teacher, Shaykh Muftī Saiful Islām Sāhib for making me part of this remarkable piece of writing. May Allāh ﷻ elevate his rank and reward him immensely in this life and the Hereafter, Āmīn.

Āyesha Khizer
JKN Graduate
April 2020 / Sha'bān 1441

Introduction to the Sūrah Al-Fath

Imagine the Prophet ﷺ encountering the trials and tribulations of the ordeals of life's toil and struggle, revolving around and enduring what would have felt comparable to an almost stationary point in existence. As a result of being impeded and suppressed every time, he ascended in climbing the ladder of achieving his hope and vision. Despite this, the Prophet ﷺ remained undeterred and continued working tirelessly, with the small band of followers who were devoted to his cause, despite the onslaught of the aggressive and violent battles they found themselves confined within the sustained succession.

This effort was not in vain as the Prophet's ﷺ endeavour was in recognition accelerated to encompass the whole of Arabia, converting to the newly found faith and he was raised to a station of praise and honour by Allāh ﷻ Himself; to heights and glory he could never imagine possible. The victory was swift, taking rapid effect as it swept across the whole of Arabia, gaining momentum and converting the masses through the beauty of its noble teachings.

This Sūrah is a Madani Sūrah, being revealed in Madīnah Munawwarah. It consists of 29 verses and four Rukūs. It was revealed after the Prophet ﷺ had migrated to Madīnah Munawwarah in the sixth year of Hijrī. The Sūrah reveals the victory Allāh ﷻ endowed upon the Prophet Muhammad ﷺ in the guise of a peace treaty which later became the reason through which the majority of the disbelievers accepted Islām.

When the Prophet ﷺ first agreed to the conditions of the treaty, many of the Sahābah ؓ felt that the treaty was unjust and unfavourable to the Muslims. Despite their own reservations, when the Prophet ﷺ went ahead and signed the Treaty of Hudaybiyah, the Sahābah ؓ stood behind the Prophet ﷺ in full support even though they could not fully comprehend the wisdom behind this decision.

This unwavering support also gained acceptance in the eyes of Allāh ﷻ, which resulted in revelation descending showing Allāh's ﷻ pleasure on the Sahābah ؓ for their unswerving commitment and matchless devotion, in obeying the Prophet ﷺ.

Throughout the journey of the Prophet's ﷺ mission, the Sahābah ؓ stood firm and steadfast in defending and protecting the Prophet ﷺ. In recognition of their hardships and struggles Allāh ﷻ sent them glad tidings of being pleased with them.

This Sūrah reflects the weakening power of the disbelievers as the believers gained the upper stronghold. The disbelievers had no choice but to conclude a treaty in recognition of the rising power of the newly found faith. The concealed evil thoughts and intentions harboured against the Prophet ﷺ and the believers by the hypocrites are also exposed. They are warned of the punishment that awaited them in the Hereafter; that their fate had been sealed by Allāh's ﷻ curse and from this, there would be no escape for them.

The Sūrah continues in conveying the message that those who disbe-lieve will suffer the consequences of their actions by being confront-ed with the eternal blaze.

The hypocrites relayed the misconception thinking that they would be able to fool the Prophet ﷺ into not joining the army by making excuses but would then be at the forefront when it came to reaping the reward in receiving the booty and treasures that were left behind.

To the sheer and utter disappointment of the hypocrites, Allāh ﷻ halted them in their tracks when He revealed the verse stating that only those who would be entitled to march forth in collecting the spoils of war, would be those who had marched forward with the Prophet ﷺ previously. Even when they attempted to stir pity into the hearts of the believers, so that perhaps they would feel a little in-clined to share part of the booty, again, this fell on deaf ears and the hypocrites were confronted with facing the loss as a result of their deceitful ploy.

There was another group who were sincere and genuine in their commitment, but as a result of suffering from one form of disability or another, they were unable to accompany the Sahābah ؓ to the battlefield. Allāh ﷻ absolved them from all guilt and blame as they would be on the same status and level of those who went out to fight had it not been for their disability.

Moreover, we see the effects of this blessing take hold after the reve-lation of the verse promising victory. The Muslims went from strength to strength; winning over the masses in a very short time, until a vast number of lands and empires were conquered; coming under the fold and domain of Islām.

The Start of Sūrah Al-Fath

The Sūrah commences with the following verse:

إِنَّا فَتَحْنَا لَكَ فَتْحًا مُّبِينًا

"Indeed We have given you (O Muhammad) a clear conquest." (48:1)

Before this verse had been revealed, the Prophet ﷺ had a dream that he was performing Umrah. A dream which is seen by a prophet is a glimpse of the future which will come to pass. After hearing about the dream, an enthusiastic group of 1400 Sahābah ؓ rallied together hoping to accompany the beloved Prophet ﷺ on this noble and unique journey.

Six long years had passed since the Sahābah ؓ had been driven out of Makkah Mukarramah. They longed to lay their eyes once again on the Holy Ka'bah. This in itself was to be a very moving and emotional journey as the Prophet ﷺ set out on this journey with the 1400 eager spirited Sahābah ؓ.

After travelling for so long on their journey, just as they had almost finally arrived, their journey took a twist. They found themselves grounded to a halt. The Sahābah ﷺ had put on their Ihrām and had brought their sacrificial animals with them to signify that they had come with no other intention other than to perform Umrah. Despite this, the disbelievers thought otherwise.

Sayyidunā Khālid Ibn Al-Walīd ﷺ, who had not yet embraced Islām at the time, had gone to intercept the believers with a group of disbelievers. At that moment, the time of Zuhr prayer had commenced and the Muslims were praying their Salāh. As they finished their prayers, Sayyidunā Khālid Ibn Al-Walīd ﷺ complained about the golden opportunity they had lost to ambush the Muslims while they prayed and so conspired that this would be fulfilled at the next prayer time.

This was not to be as Allāh ﷻ sent a revelation warning the Prophet ﷺ that in cases where their lives were endangered, they should pray the Salāh of Fear so that half the number of people could pray while the other half stood guard, and then they would take it in turns until the Salāh was completed. Thus the effort of the disbelievers was foiled. This is explained in the following verse:

وَإِذَا كُنتَ فِيهِمْ فَأَقَمْتَ لَهُمُ الصَّلَاةَ فَلْتَقُمْ طَآئِفَةٌ مِّنْهُم مَّعَكَ وَلْيَأْخُذُوٓا أَسْلِحَتَهُمْ فَإِذَا سَجَدُوا فَلْيَكُونُوا مِن وَرَآئِكُمْ وَلْتَأْتِ طَآئِفَةٌ أُخْرَىٰ لَمْ يُصَلُّوا فَلْيُصَلُّوا مَعَكَ وَلْيَأْخُذُوا حِذْرَهُمْ وَأَسْلِحَتَهُمْ ۗ وَدَّ الَّذِينَ كَفَرُوا لَوْ تَغْفُلُونَ عَنْ أَسْلِحَتِكُمْ وَأَمْتِعَتِكُمْ فَيَمِيلُونَ عَلَيْكُم مَّيْلَةً وَاحِدَةً ۚ وَلَا جُنَاحَ عَلَيْكُمْ إِن كَانَ بِكُمْ أَذًى مِّن مَّطَرٍ أَوْ كُنتُم مَّرْضَىٰ أَن

تَضَعُوٓاْ أَسْلِحَتَكُمْ ۖ وَخُذُواْ حِذْرَكُمْ ۗ إِنَّ اللَّهَ أَعَدَّ لِلْكَٰفِرِينَ عَذَابًا مُّهِينًا

"And when you are among them and lead them in prayer, let a group of them stand (in prayer) with you and let them carry their arms. And when they have prostrated, let them be (in position) behind you and have the other group come forward which has not (yet) prayed and let them pray with you, taking precaution and carrying their arms. Those who disbelieve wish that you would neglect your weapons so they could come down upon you in (one) single attack. But there is no blame upon you, if you are troubled by rain or are ill, for putting down your arms, but take precaution. Indeed, Allāh has prepared for the disbelievers a humiliating punishment." (4:102)

As the Sahābah ﷺ had come to perform Umrah, they had not carried arms; only their traveller's swords. Although this verse was revealed to guide them in this situation, the general guideline is still applicable for all times and all ages. Even though they had not brought their weapons, they still had to stand in defence through whatever means were at their disposal.

Types of Dreams

As mentioned, before the revelation of Sūrah Al-Fath, the Prophet ﷺ had seen a dream in which he was performing Umrah. In relation to this, there are three types of dreams:

1. Rahmāni Dreams - these are from Allāh ﷻ. An example of this is a person seeing a dream giving them glad tidings of Jannah. This should be a source of comfort. However, if a person decided that because of this dream, all sense of restrictions and obligations on them has been lifted and no longer apply, then they will only deceive themselves.

When the Prophet ﷺ was given glad tidings that any past and future mistakes of his were forgiven, this only led to him further increasing his efforts. Sayyidunā Mughīrah Ibn Shu'bah ﷺ reported the Prophet ﷺ would pray until his feet were swollen. It was said, "Why do you do this when Allāh ﷻ has forgiven your past and future mistakes?" The Prophet ﷺ replied, "Shall I not be a grateful servant?" (Muslim)

The fact that the Prophet ﷺ had seen himself in a dream performing Umrah meant that this would inevitably take place because the Prophet's ﷺ dreams were revelations. This is similar to the dream of Prophet Ibrāhīm عليه السلام who saw himself sacrificing his son as mentioned in the Qur'ān:

$$ فَلَمَّا بَلَغَ مَعَهُ السَّعْىَ قَالَ يٰبُنَىَّ إِنِّىٓ أَرٰى فِى الْمَنَامِ أَنِّىٓ أَذْبَحُكَ فَانْظُرْ مَاذَا تَرٰى ۚ قَالَ يٰٓأَبَتِ افْعَلْ مَا تُؤْمَرُ ۖ سَتَجِدُنِىٓ إِنْ شَآءَ اللّٰهُ مِنَ الصّٰبِرِيْنَ $$

"And when he reached with him (the age of) exertion he said, 'O my son; I have seen in a dream that I (must) sacrifice you, so see what you think.' He said, 'O my father, do as you are commanded. You will find me, if Allāh wills, of the steadfast." (37:102)

In the case of Sayyidunā Ibrāhīm ﷺ, he was ready and willing to obey his Lord in satisfying the criteria set out to test his faith and commitment through the revelation of divine dreams. First this was to leave his son in the desert and then to sacrifice him.

2. Nafsāni Dreams - these type of dreams occur due to a person's imagination and own thoughts.

3. Shaytāni Dreams - for example, wet dreams. These type of dreams are from the Shaytān.

A dream itself is not a proof of divine instruction for an ordinary person, rather specific criteria and standards have to be met before a dream can be classified as being a truthful vision.

The Blockade

The disbelievers had gathered and not only were they refusing the believers to continue with their journey, but they were also prevented from entering Makkah Mukarramah in order for them to perform their Umrah. In doing so, they also prevented the Prophet ﷺ and his followers from sacrificing the 70 animals they had brought with them.

The Prophet ﷺ sought advice and Sayyidunā Abū Bakr ﷺ stated that they had not come to fight but to perform Umrah and if the disbelievers persisted in preventing them, only then they should fight them.

Urwah Ibn Mas'ūd was one of the leaders of the Quraysh who had not yet accepted Islām. He approached the Prophet ﷺ and tried to reason with him and explain how futile all this fighting had become, which had only caused the army of the disbelievers to be weakened.

The Prophet ﷺ explained that if they ceased fighting, they could join them in battling the rest of the Arabs, which meant that if they succeeded, then victory would be for both sides. If they disagreed at that time, then they could battle it out, but at that present moment in time they had only come to perform Umrah and so wished to be allowed to continue without a struggle.

As Urwah Ibn Mas'ūd observed and watched, he was much impressed by what he saw. After returning to Makkah Mukarramah, he informed the leaders regarding what he had seen and described how the Sahābah ﵉ honour and respect the Prophet ﷺ. He said, "I have visited the Kings of Persia, Rome and Abyssinia but I have not seen any leader more revered and respected than Muhammad. If he ordered his followers to do anything, they do it without delay. If he performs ablution, they all seek the remainder of the water he used. They never look at him in the eyes out of respect for him."

The Reverence of the Sahābah ﷺ

According to the narration of Sayyidunā Barā Ibn Āzib ﷺ, "There was a shortage of water in the well of Hudaybiyah. There was not even a drop of water remaining in the well. The situation was relayed to the Prophet Muhammad ﷺ. Prophet Muhammad ﷺ came to the side of the well and sat down. He wanted a pot filled with a little water. After he made Wudhū with the water they (the Sahābah) brought to him, he rinsed his mouth and prayed silently. He poured the water which he used for making Wudhū into the well. With the permission of the Prophet ﷺ, the well was left alone. Then, the well had water. Both the Muslims and their animals drank from that well. 1400 people drank from the water of that well." (Bukhāri)

The above Hadīth explains that on one occasion the Sahābah ﷺ needed to perform Wudhū but the well they had come across was completely dry. The Prophet ﷺ prayed to Allāh ﷻ and after he had rinsed his mouth and poured the water into the well alongside the water he had used to perform Wudhū, the well filled up with water.

The Prophet's ﷺ saliva was full of blessings. When the Prophet ﷺ rinsed his mouth, the Sahābah ﷺ would rush to collect the water and anoint their faces, Subhān-Allāh! How could a person not be left mesmerised after observing and watching the Prophet ﷺ performing Wudhū (ablution) as the blessed drops of water fell from his hands and limbs. It was almost as if the Sahābah ﷺ were fighting with one another to catch the trickles and drops, and with that they would rub their faces and entire body. Those that missed out would rub their hands over the hands of the Sahābah ☙ who had caught the drops in order to seek the blessings of the ablution water left behind by the Prophet 🕮.

Other Companions ☙ would even adopt eating whatever the Prophet 🕮 would eat to the extent that they made it their favourite food.

Sayyidunā Anas ☙ narrates, "A person invited Allāh's Messenger 🕮 to a meal. I also went along with him. He brought soup containing pumpkin. Allāh's Messenger 🕮 ate that pumpkin with relish. He (Anas) said, 'When I saw that I began to place it before him and did not eat it (myself). It was since then that pumpkin was always my favourite (food)." From that day onwards Sayyidunā Anas ☙ states that pumpkin became his favourite food to this extent that he never had a dish which did not contain pumpkin in it.

The reverence and awe the Sahābah ☙ had for the Prophet 🕮 surpassed every expectation of respect, admiration and approval. This did not go unnoticed amongst the polytheists of Makkah Mukarramah as mentioned earlier about Urwah Ibn Mas'ūd. Although he had not converted to Islām at the time, he tried to prevent the polytheists from fighting the Muslims.

Envoy after envoy were sent, but every one of them came back with identical corresponding reports that the Muslims had only come on peaceful grounds and did not intend to cause any uproar or conflict.

The polytheists of Makkah Mukarramah on the other hand were dissatisfied with the outcome of what was happening. They recruited 50 people and decided that they would assassinate the Prophet ﷺ.

Assassination Plot

Sayyidunā Muhammad Ibn Maslamah ﷺ protected the Prophet ﷺ, in that he was able to capture the fifty people and foil their plans. After much deliberation, the Prophet ﷺ finally decided to send Sayyidunā Uthmān ﷺ to speak to the polytheists. As he entered into Makkah Mukarramah, he saw the pitiful plight of the Muslims who remained behind in captivity and reassured them that their suffering would soon be alleviated by the will of Allāh ﷻ.

As the polytheists conversed with Sayyidunā Uthmān ﷺ, they allowed him the opportunity to perform Umrah. At once, he declined and rejected the offer expressing his horror at the very thought of himself performing Umrah while the Prophet ﷺ was prevented entry into the Holy City. This was out of the deep love he felt for the Prophet ﷺ that he took this course of action. Never could he even imagine, let alone contemplate in carrying out something that the Prophet ﷺ himself was prevented from performing.

Bay'atur Ridhwān

Sayyidunā Uthmān ﷺ had been delayed from returning. During this time a rumour had spread that he had been killed. The Prophet ﷺ gathered the Sahābah ﷺ under a tree and took the pledge of allegiance from them that they would fight to avenge the death of Sayyidunā Uthmān ﷺ. This pledge was known as *'Bay'at ur Ridhwān'*.

1400 Sahābah ﷺ took the pledge of allegiance. One Sahābi, Sayyidunā Salamah Ibn Al-Akwa ﷺ had the privilege of reaffirming his pledge of allegiance three times at the hands of the Prophet ﷺ. This blessing manifested itself in Sayyidunā Salamah Ibn Al-Akwa ﷺ who possessed agility that was inexhaustible, becoming known as the fastest man capable of outrunning horses.

This pledge pleased Allāh ﷻ to the point that He revealed a verse regarding those who took it to confirm that He was pleased with them:

$$لَقَدْ رَضِيَ اللهُ عَنِ الْمُؤْمِنِينَ إِذْ يُبَايِعُونَكَ تَحْتَ الشَّجَرَةِ فَعَلِمَ مَا فِي قُلُوبِهِمْ فَأَنْزَلَ السَّكِينَةَ عَلَيْهِمْ وَأَثَابَهُمْ فَتْحًا قَرِيبًا$$

"Certainly Allāh was pleased with the believers when they pledged allegiance to you, (O Muhammad) under the tree, and He knew what was in their hearts, so He sent down tranquillity upon them and rewarded them with an imminent conquest." (48:18)

21

This is the standard and rank that Sahābah Kirām ﷺ gained in Allāh's ﷻ sight and yet there are those today who attempt to criticise and belittle them in a very reviling manner.

The 1400 Sahābah Kirām ﷺ who pledged allegiance to the Prophet ﷺ were given glad tidings of Paradise. The Prophet ﷺ himself put his own hand forth in pledging allegiance on behalf of Sayyidunā Uthmān ﷺ. The pledge demonstrated the determination and firmness of the Muslims.

News spread that the Muslims were getting ready to attack and it was on this occasion, the polytheists of Makkah decided that it would serve their best interests to release Sayyidunā Uthmān ﷺ and enter into a peace treaty with the Muslims.

It was only after this that the polytheists sent Suhail Ibn Amr as an ambassador to negotiate the terms of the peace treaty, which came to be known as the Treaty of Hudaybiyah.

The Peace Treaty of Hudaybiyah

Suhail Ibn Amr was sent as the chief negotiator to the Muslims. As he commenced the peace treaty, the Prophet ﷺ asked the scribe to write down the words, 'In the name of Allāh, the Beneficent, the Most Merciful.'

Suhail Ibn Amr immediately objected to this saying that he recognised no such deity with these attributes and so the Prophet ﷺ agreed to just write, "Bismik Allāhumma." The scribe, Sayyidunā Alī ؓ had also written 'the Messenger of Allāh' to which Suhail Ibn Amr also opposed. When Sayyidunā Alī ؓ refused to erase it because of the deep love he had for the Prophet ﷺ, the Prophet ﷺ himself erased it with his own hands after having been shown where the words were written as the Prophet ﷺ was unlettered. He then agreed to write, "Muhammad Ibn Abdullāh" in its place in agreement with the polytheists.

The peace treaty stipulated that there would be a truce for ten years so people could live side by side in peace and interact with one another freely. The polytheists also included that the Muslims would have to return that year and come back the following year to perform Umrah and they would not be allowed to stay for more than three days. They felt that by allowing the Muslims to go ahead with Umrah at that point would convey a message that the disbelievers had been defeated and the Muslims were triumphant. This is something that they would never allow to happen.

Another condition set forth was that any of their people who decided to migrate to Madīnah Munawwarah, would have to be returned. However, if anyone decided to leave the Muslims and go back to Makkah Mukarramah, they would not be returned. If anyone wished to form alliances with any other group, they would be free to do so from both sides. Immediately, the tribe of Banū Khuzā'ah joined the

Prophet ﷺ while the tribe of Banū Bakr joined the Quraysh.

As the treaty was being concluded, Sayyidunā Abū Jandal ؓ, who was the son of the person who was negotiating the treaty, came amid the Muslims somehow managing to free himself from the chains that he had been restrained in.

He pleaded with the Prophet ﷺ to accept him in his group, stating the suffering and ordeal he had endured. The Prophet ﷺ requested Suhail Ibn Amr to allow Sayyidunā Abū Jandal ؓ to join the Muslims as the treaty had not yet been signed but he refused stating that if they chose to take his son, then there would be no peace treaty.

The Prophet ﷺ gently spoke to Sayyidunā Abū Jandal ؓ assuring him that his patience would not be in vain and that he should continue forbearing his circumstances and ease would soon follow with the will of Allāh ﷻ.

Broken Treaty and the Conquest of Makkah Mukarramah

After the treaty was formed, they were told to leave and had to return to Madīnah Munawwarah. On their return the following blessed verse was revealed:

$$\text{إِنَّا فَتَحْنَا لَكَ فَتْحًا مُّبِينًا}$$

"Indeed We have given you (O Muhammad) a clear con-

quest." (48:1)

The initial thought after this verse was revealed was one of confusion and bewilderment. Many of the Sahābah ﷺ, alongside Sayyidunā Umar ﷺ, could not comprehend how a one-sided peace treaty and the humiliation of being sent back without the ability to perform Umrah could be signs of a victory and triumph. The feelings of being dispirited and downcast ran high but Allāh ﷻ proved them otherwise with the complete change and transformation that followed within a short period of two years.

The peace treaty of Hudaybiyah was known as Al-Fath (the victory) because this was the stepping stone that paved the way for a landslide victory in which the overwhelming masses converted to Islām.

The Prophet ﷺ had the opportunity to invite people to Islām from wide and afar; writing letters to the Kings, leaders and governors of the vast surrounding territories. Restrictions on travel were uplifted so that the Muslims could, for the very first time, move about freely without fearing the threat to their lives. Within the short period of two years, the Muslim army had gone from 1400 strong to a force of 10,000 men at the conquest of Makkah Mukarramah.

The peace treaty of Hudaybiyah was broken two years later when a person from the tribe of Banū Bakr allied with the polytheists and killed a person from the tribe of Banū Khuzā'ah, who was allied with the Muslims. This then led to the Prophet ﷺ marching on with his army of men which resulted in the conquest of Makkah Mukarramah in the 8th year of Hijri. This promised victory was given to the Prophet ﷺ and the Sahābah ؓ.

Three Rewards Given to the Prophet ﷺ

In addition to the conquest of Makkah Mukarramah, the Prophet ﷺ was given a further three rewards:

The first reward was that Allāh ﷻ declared that all the Prophet's ﷺ mistakes of the past, present and future were all forgiven.

The Ahlus Sunnah Wal Jamā'at believe that all the Prophets are sinless. Every blemish, major or minor was cleansed and washed away whether it was carried out before or after Prophethood. Allāh ﷻ has protected them which is explained in the following verse:

$$لِيَغْفِرَ لَكَ اللّٰهُ مَا تَقَدَّمَ مِنْ ذَنْبِكَ وَمَا تَأَخَّرَ وَيُتِمَّ نِعْمَتَهُ عَلَيْكَ وَيَهْدِيَكَ صِرَاطًا مُّسْتَقِيْمًا$$

"That Allāh may forgive for you what preceded of your sin and what will follow and complete His favour upon you and guide you to a straight path." (48:2)

The 'sins' that is being referred to here are misjudgements that Allāh ﷻ forgave him for. They were above committing sins commonly perpetrated by the common people because they were above any ordinary standard, unrivalled in their conduct and behaviour.

An example of the Prophet's ﷺ misjudgement is in the Battle of Badr. After the battle had ended, the Muslims found themselves faced with a large number of prisoners of war. After consulting with the Sahābah ؓ, it was decided that they would exchange the prisoners of war for ransom, when it would have been more proper that the disbelievers were thoroughly subdued. This is because the enemy would prove to be treacherous and join the fight against the Muslims again due to their deep-rooted enmity for the believers.

The Prophet ﷺ is addressed by Allāh ﷻ that even though he had exchanged the prisoners of war out of compassion, there had been an oversight in his judgement. However, Allāh ﷻ had overlooked his misjudgement which is further elucidated in the following verse:

مَا كَانَ لِنَبِيٍّ أَنْ يَّكُوْنَ لَهُ أَسْرَى حَتّٰى يُثْخِنَ فِي الْأَرْضِ ۚ تُرِيْدُوْنَ عَرَضَ الدُّنْيَا ۖ وَاللّٰهُ يُرِيْدُ
الْأٰخِرَةَ ۗ وَاللّٰهُ عَزِيْزٌ حَكِيْمٌ

"It is not befitting a prophet that he has captives with him unless he has subdued the enemy by shedding blood in the land. You intend to have the stuff of this world, while Allāh intends the Hereafter (for you). And Allāh is All-Mighty, All-Wise." (8:67)

What we have to take into consideration is that these polytheists were bent on uprooting Islām and they would have left no stone unturned in eradicating the faith if such an opportunity arose.

By exchanging the prisoners for ransom, this would have provided the disbelievers with more ammunition to attack the believers.

Therefore the threat would have become critical and much more severe. The battle represented the demarcation between truth and falsehood and on these grounds falsehood had to be eradicated.

It was a trying and testing time for the believers who found themselves up against their own kinsmen. For many, each time they glanced across, their own fathers, brothers and uncles were visible within the ranks of the disbelievers, but despite this, it did not deter them when it came to distinguishing between truth and falsehood.

The ties of kinship became severed when the threat of Islām being destroyed by their own kinsmen lay looming in the horizon. Moreover, the Sahābah ﷺ proved themselves to the extent that when they were fighting the enemy, no distinction was made between the enemy ranks, be it their own father or brother.

It is because of this that Allāh ﷻ turned to them in compassion and forgave them their mistakes. This was also to prove fruitful because amongst them, there were many who up until this point, had not witnessed the true brotherhood and love for their fellow human being that Islām represented. This led to many of the prisoners of war accepting Islām when they were made to witness such behaviour during their captivity.

For 13 long years, the Prophet ﷺ and his Companions ﷺ tolerated the suffering and persecution of the idolaters without resorting to arms despite facing fierce opposition and extensive brutality. They

toiled on with patience and forbearance. This only led to further es-
calation of violence and savagery against them until they were left
with no choice but to defend themselves as instructed by Allāh 🌸 in
the Qur'ān.

Islām is not a passive religion. A person's blood, honour and property are sacred in Islām and any attack has to be resisted and repressed
to eliminate oppression, persecution and maltreatment. Sometimes
the appointed methods are necessitated if the outcome is to be successful in accomplishing peace in society. This can be seen across all
national and geographical borders. Every country has arms to defend itself from enemy attacks and this is necessary if evil is to remain subdued. Rules and regulations have to be in place and en-
forced if necessary to ensure the smooth running of a peaceful and
prosperous society.

The immoral behaviour of a few can cause great suffering to many
and to protect the members of society rules are set in motion. As
much as we wish to live in security and peace, at the same time, we
cannot remain unplanned for the possible threat and danger that exists in our community and the world at large.

Many proclaim that resorting to arms is not the answer and we
should always seek to derive peaceful methods in solving a problem.
This would be ideal if we were not faced with people who are truly
wicked and lawless; driven by their contemptible and abominable
behaviour into committing heinous atrocities. If these people are not
averted and stopped by the use of force, then the outcome would be

dire as explained in the Qur'ān:

وَلَوْلَا دَفْعُ اللّٰهِ النَّاسَ بَعْضَهُم بِبَعْضٍ لَّفَسَدَتِ الْأَرْضُ وَلٰكِنَّ اللّٰهَ ذُو فَضْلٍ عَلَى الْعَالَمِيْنَ

**"And if it were not for Allāh checking (some) people by means
of others, the earth would have been corrupted, but Allāh is full
of bounty to the worlds." (2:251)**

The hypocrites were another group who professed belief with their
tongues but not in their hearts. When they came into the presence
of the Prophet ﷺ just moments before the time of the battle, they
would put forward their excuses saying that their houses were exposed and their womenfolk were in danger. On one occasion the
Prophet ﷺ accepted their excuses and allowed them to stay behind.
However, Allāh ﷻ exposed their evil and reproached the Prophet ﷺ
explaining that he should not have exempted them from the fighting.
This is further elucidated in the following verse:

عَفَا اللّٰهُ عَنكَ لِمَ أَذِنْتَ لَهُمْ حَتّٰى يَتَبَيَّنَ لَكَ الَّذِيْنَ صَدَقُوا وَتَعْلَمَ الْكَاذِبِيْنَ

**"May Allāh pardon you, (O Muhammad); Why did you give
them permission (to remain behind)? (You should not have) until it was evident to you who were truthful and you knew (who
were) the liars." (9:43)**

The second attribute given to the Prophet ﷺ was that Allāh ﷻ guided him to the straight path and his position would continue to be
elevated. Allāh ﷻ says:

وَرَفَعْنَا لَكَ ذِكْرَكَ

"And We raised high your name." (94:4)

There are numerous stages of Hidāyat (guidance). For a disbeliever, entering the fold of Islām is Hidāyat. When we pray our Salāh, we ask for Hidāyat, when we say:

اِهْدِنَا الصِّرَاطَ الْمُسْتَقِيْمَ

By saying *"Ihdinas sirātal mustaqīm,"* (Guide us along the straight path) we are asking Allāh ﷻ to keep us firm on the Dīn and not to allow our hearts to deviate after receiving guidance.

The third attribute that was given to the Prophet ﷺ was divine help, as mentioned in the following verse:

وَيَنْصُرَكَ اللّٰهُ نَصْرًا عَزِيْزًا

"And (that) Allāh may aid you with a mighty victory." (48:3)

Allāh ﷻ addresses the Prophet ﷺ to continue in his mission and guarantees him with divine assistance. Allāh ﷻ addresses the people saying that even if they chose not to help the Prophet ﷺ, then Allāh ﷻ Himself would assist him similar to when the Prophet ﷺ sought refuge in a cave while the disbelievers stood outside. If they had only just looked down, they would have seen the Prophet ﷺ but Allāh ﷻ protected him and the idolaters were thrown off course. Allāh ﷻ

says:

$$\text{إِلَّا تَنْصُرُوهُ فَقَدْ نَصَرَهُ اللّٰهُ إِذْ أَخْرَجَهُ الَّذِيْنَ كَفَرُوا ثَانِيَ اثْنَيْنِ إِذْ هُمَا فِي الْغَارِ إِذْ يَقُوْلُ لِصَاحِبِهِ لَا تَحْزَنْ إِنَّ اللّٰهَ مَعَنَا ۚ فَأَنْزَلَ اللّٰهُ سَكِيْنَتَهُ عَلَيْهِ وَأَيَّدَهُ بِجُنُوْدٍ لَّمْ تَرَوْهَا وَجَعَلَ كَلِمَةَ الَّذِيْنَ كَفَرُوا السُّفْلَىٰ ۗ وَكَلِمَةُ اللّٰهِ هِيَ الْعُلْيَا ۗ وَاللّٰهُ عَزِيْزٌ حَكِيْمٌ}$$

"If you do not aid the Prophet, Allāh had already aided him when those who disbelieved had driven him out (of Makkah) as one of two when they were in the cave and he said to his Companion, 'Do not grieve; Indeed Allāh is with us.' And Allāh sent down His tranquillity upon him and supported him with angels, you did not see and made the word of those who disbelieved the lowest, while the word of Allāh; that is the highest. And Allāh is Exalted in Might and Wise." (9:40)

It is narrated that Sayyidunā Abū Bakr ﷺ said, "I said to the Prophet ﷺ when I was with him in the cave, 'If one of them looks down at his feet, he will see us.' He said, 'What do you think O Abū Bakr, of two the third of whom is Allāh?'" (Bukhārī)

Within a short space of 10 years, Islām had spread throughout the land and consequently the whole of Arabia had come under the banner of Islām.

When studying the Sīrah of the Prophet ﷺ, one will reach the conclusion that this success could not have come about without divine intervention. The first battle that the Prophet ﷺ took part in; the

Battle of Badr consisted of 313 ill-equipped men, two horses and 70 camels fighting against 1000 well-equipped soldiers. Yet, Allāh ﷻ granted them swift victory to the utter shock and dismay of the enemies.

When the Prophet ﷺ recited the verses which spoke about the merits attributed to him, the Sahābah ؓ congratulated him and then asked: "What is for us, what are we going to get?" Allāh ﷻ then revealed:

هُوَ الَّذِيٓ أَنْزَلَ السَّكِينَةَ فِي قُلُوبِ الْمُؤْمِنِينَ لِيَزْدَادُوٓا إِيمَانًا مَّعَ إِيمَانِهِمْ ۗ وَلِلَّهِ جُنُودُ السَّمَٰوَٰتِ وَالْأَرْضِ ۚ وَكَانَ اللَّهُ عَلِيمًا حَكِيمًا

"It is He Who sent down tranquillity into the hearts of the believers that they would increase in faith along with their (present) faith. And to Allāh belong the soldiers of the heavens and the earth and ever is Allāh Knowing and Wise." (48:4)

Allāh ﷻ sent down tranquillity in the form of inner serenity and contentment that filled the hearts of the believers in strengthening their faith further.

Remembrance of Allāh ﷻ and Inner Peace

These traits and qualities of strong faith and a content heart are something that we lack so much today. Despite mankind having greater monetary wealth and power, inner peace and tranquillity are far from being achieved and established.

This only gives further weight to the notion that no amount of physical gain can bring us true happiness if inner contentment and harmony is not present within. Allāh ﷻ says:

اَلَّذِيْنَ اٰمَنُوْا وَتَطْمَئِنُّ قُلُوْبُهُمْ بِذِكْرِ اللهِ ۗ اَلَا بِذِكْرِ اللهِ تَطْمَئِنُّ الْقُلُوْبُ

"Those who have believed and whose hearts are assured by the remembrance of Allāh. Unquestionably, by the remembrance of Allāh hearts are assured." (13:28)

Regarding those who turn away from the remembrance of Allāh ﷻ, He says:

وَمَنْ اَعْرَضَ عَنْ ذِكْرِيْ فَاِنَّ لَهٗ مَعِيْشَةً ضَنْكًا وَّنَحْشُرُهٗ يَوْمَ الْقِيَامَةِ اَعْمٰى

"And whoever turns away from My Remembrance, indeed, he will have a depressed life and We will gather him on the Day of Resurrection blind." (20:124)

Remembrance here refers to following Allāh's ﷻ commands and orders.

The punishment on the Day of Judgement will also be severe. The person will be raised blind. He will then question as to why he is in such a condition and Allāh ﷻ will answer:

قَالَ كَذٰلِكَ اَتَتْكَ اٰيٰتُنَا فَنَسِيْتَهَا ۚ وَكَذٰلِكَ الْيَوْمَ تُنْسٰى ﴿١٢٦﴾ وَكَذٰلِكَ نَجْزِيْ مَنْ اَسْرَفَ

وَلَمْ يُؤْمِنْ بِـَٔايَٰتِ رَبِّهِ ۚ وَلَعَذَابُ ٱلْءَاخِرَةِ أَشَدُّ وَأَبْقَىٰ ﴿١٢٧﴾

"He will say, 'My Lord, why have You raised me blind while I was (once) seeing?' (Allāh) will say, ' Thus did Our signs come to you, and you forgot them; and thus will you this Day be forgotten'. And thus do We recompense he who transgressed and did not believe in the signs of his Lord. And the punishment of the Hereafter is more severe and more enduring." (20:126-127)

Further to this, the Prophet ﷺ said, *"Whoever misses the Jumuah Salāh three times on account of negligence, then Allāh will put a seal on his heart."* (Tirmidhī, Abū Dāwūd).

Allāh ﷻ stamps their heart so that no goodness enters. This is the severity regarding turning away from just this one example of Allāh's ﷻ orders. Divine assistance and help to enable one to carry out good deeds will be withdrawn. We see many who are in this position. When Dīn is mentioned, the person is averse to heed any advice. Our Dīn comes first. If we are in such a workplace that cannot accommodate for our necessity to pray, then it is impermissible for us to continue with that position.

The Pledge of Allegiance

After 1400 Sahābah ؓ pledged allegiance to the Prophet ﷺ, they were given glad tidings that they would be saved from entering the punishment of the Hellfire.

لَقَدْ رَضِيَ اللهُ عَنِ الْمُؤْمِنِينَ إِذْ يُبَايِعُونَكَ تَحْتَ الشَّجَرَةِ فَعَلِمَ مَا فِي قُلُوبِهِمْ فَأَنْزَلَ السَّكِينَةَ عَلَيْهِمْ وَأَثَابَهُمْ فَتْحًا قَرِيبًا

"Certainly Allāh was pleased with the believers when they pledged allegiance to you (O Muhammad) under the tree and He knew what was in their hearts, so He sent down tranquillity upon them and rewarded them with an imminent conquest." (48:18)

Sayyidunā Abū Hurairah ؓ reported that the Messenger of Allāh ﷺ said, *"The world is a prison for the believer and a paradise for the disbeliever." (Muslim)*

When inner peace and contentment enters the heart, no amount of pain or suffering, however great can take this tranquillity away. Sayyidunā Bilāl ؓ is an illustrious example of what happens when a person tastes the sweetness of faith. He was brutally tortured and made to lie on the scorching heat of the desert sand with a large boulder on his chest to force him to renounce his faith. However despite these conditions, he continued to say *'Ahad Ahad'* (The One, The One)!

How powerful the words of belief are as our beloved Prophet ﷺ explained of uttering the words *'Lā ilāha illallāh'*, (There is no god but Allāh ﷻ).

When Sayyidunā Mūsā ؑ asked Allāh ﷻ to teach him something

36

unique, Allāh ﷻ told him to say, '*Lā ilāha illallāh*' saying that if the seven heavens and the seven earths and all that it contains were placed on one side of the scale and '*Lā ilāha illallāh*' on the other, the side with '*Lā ilāha illallāh*' would be heavier.

Something we can so easily recite with our tongues but despite knowing this, there will be many of us who will still remain idle and impassive to the words of Allāh ﷻ. What could be a greater sense of loss than this in failing to reap such easy rewards?

When the Treaty of Hudaybiyah was drawn, the Sahābah ؓ felt that injustice had been committed. This was because they felt that it was a one-sided peace treaty and were eager to re-address the wrong by engaging in battle. Allāh ﷻ in His wisdom prevented this through His Prophet ﷺ.

All Knowing, All Wise

In verse four of this Sūrah, Allāh ﷻ describes himself as عَلِيمًا حَكِيمًا (*Alīman Hakīmā*) which is the Knowing, the Wise. This demonstrates that despite Allāh ﷻ having every army at His disposal to attack those who seek to transgress, yet He is also the Wise and will do so in His own timing and at His own discretion.

If Allāh ﷻ wants to take swift and abrupt action He could easily do so, such as when He destroyed Abrahah and his army when they had come to destroy the Ka'bah, or when He sent violent winds which destroyed countless nations such as the Tribe of Ād for their acts of transgression.

At times we may be compelled to partake in something that we feel is hopeless, yet Allāh ﷻ has kept much good in it for us. On the other hand, we may be inclined to take a course of action which although may appear fruitful, has great harm within it. It is only through following revelation and guidance that we will be able to achieve true success and enter Jannah, as mentioned in the following verse:

لِيُدْخِلَ الْمُؤْمِنِيْنَ وَالْمُؤْمِنٰتِ جَنّٰتٍ تَجْرِيْ مِنْ تَحْتِهَا الْأَنْهٰرُ خٰلِدِيْنَ فِيْهَا وَيُكَفِّرَ عَنْهُمْ سَيِّاٰتِهِمْ ۚ وَكَانَ ذٰلِكَ عِنْدَ اللهِ فَوْزًا عَظِيْمًا

"(And) that He may admit the believing men and the believing women to gardens beneath which rivers flow to abide therein eternally and remove from them their misdeeds and ever is that, in the sight of Allāh, a great attainment." (48:5)

Hakīmul Ummah Shaykh Ashraf Alī Thānwi ﷯ used to say that after every Fardh Salāh, we should recite the following Duʿā to preserve our Īmān until our last breath:

رَبَّنَا لَا تُزِغْ قُلُوْبَنَا بَعْدَ إِذْ هَدَيْتَنَا وَهَبْ لَنَا مِنْ لَّدُنْكَ رَحْمَةً ۚ إِنَّكَ أَنْتَ الْوَهَّابُ

"Our Lord, let not our hearts deviate after You have guided us and grant us from Yourself mercy. Indeed, You are the Bestower." (3:8)

Even though we have been blessed with Īmān, we still need to make Du'ā to Allāh ﷻ that He allows it to take root and firmly establish in our hearts.

Believer in the Morning but not in the Evening

A period will come in the approach to the end of time when a person will be a believer in the morning, a disbeliever in the evening. Our own beloved Shaykh spoke of the number of people who came to him explaining that their Nikāh (marriage contract) had to be re-done on account of one of the spouses uttering statements of Kufr in a fit of anger that they did not believe in Allāh ﷻ or Islām. This would not only negate their faith but also nullify their marriage for which Nikāh would have to be repeated.

Shaykh also mentioned an incident which was dealt by Mufti Mahmūd Hasan Gangohi ﷁ, the Grand Mufti of India about a husband during an episode in a drama where he had jokingly given Talāq (divorce) to his wife. When asked what the ruling would be regarding such behaviour, Mufti Sāhib replied that let alone their marriage, even their Īmān would be at a loss because they made a mockery out of Allāh's ﷻ Dīn and Injunctions. Allāh ﷻ says in the Qur'ān:

وَلَئِن سَأَلْتَهُمْ لَيَقُولُنَّ إِنَّمَا كُنَّا نَخُوضُ وَنَلْعَبُ ۚ قُلْ أَبِاللَّهِ وَآيَاتِهِ وَرَسُولِهِ كُنتُمْ تَسْتَهْزِئُونَ ﴿٦٥﴾ لَا تَعْتَذِرُوا قَدْ كَفَرْتُم بَعْدَ إِيمَانِكُمْ ۚ إِن نَّعْفُ عَن طَائِفَةٍ مِّنكُمْ

نُعَذِّبْ طَآئِفَةً بِأَنَّهُمْ كَانُوا مُجْرِمِينَ ﴿٦٦﴾

**"And if you ask them, they will surely say, 'We were only con-
versing and playing.' Say, 'Is it Allāh and His verses and His Messenger that you were mocking.' Make no excuse; you have disbelieved after your belief. If we pardon one faction of you, We will
punish another faction because they were criminals." (9:65-66)**

Many times we blurt out speech without a moments thought to the
seriousness of what we are exclaiming. On the Day of Judgement,
many people will go forward only to be made aware of the grim reality that their Īmān has been negated and lost.

In another verse Allāh ﷻ says:

يَـٰٓأَيُّهَا الَّذِينَ ءَامَنُوٓا ءَامِنُوا بِاللّٰهِ وَرَسُولِهِ وَالْكِتَابِ الَّذِي نَزَّلَ عَلَىٰ رَسُولِهِ وَالْكِتَابِ الَّذِيٓ
أَنْزَلَ مِن قَبْلُ ۚ وَمَن يَكْفُرْ بِاللّٰهِ وَمَلَـٰٓئِكَتِهِ وَكُتُبِهِ وَرُسُلِهِ وَالْيَوْمِ الْأَخِرِ فَقَدْ ضَلَّ ضَلَالًا
بَعِيدًا

**"O you who have believed, believe in Allāh and His Messenger
and the Book He sent down upon His Messenger and the scripture which He sent down before. And whoever disbelieves in
Allāh, His Angels, His Books, His Messengers and the Last Day
has certainly gone far astray." (4:136)**

Reward of Paradise

We should remain steadfast and re-fresh our Īmān with *Lā ilāha illallāh* (There is no god but Allāh 🕮). The reward of those who ad-here to following the commands of Allāh 🕮 is explained in a Ḥadīth which has been narrated by Sayyidunā Abū Hurairah 🕮 where the Prophet 🕮 said, "Allāh 🕮 says, 'I have prepared for My righteous slaves which no eye has seen, no ear has heard and it has never crossed the mind of man.' Then he recited: **'No person knows what is kept hidden for them as joy, as a reward for what they used to do.'"** (32:17)(Bukhāri)

The rivers of Jannah will be flowing on level ground. There will be rivers of honey, wine, water and milk. The taste or composition of the rivers will never change. This will be unlimited and endless.

Regarding the rewards promised to those who will enter Paradise, Allāh 🕮 says:

$$لَهُمْ مَّا يَشَاءُوْنَ فِيْهَا وَلَدَيْنَا مَزِيْدٌ$$
"They will have whatever they wish therein and with Us is more." (50:35)

In another verse Allāh 🕮 says:

$$إِنَّ الَّذِيْنَ اٰمَنُوْا وَعَمِلُوا الصَّالِحَاتِ كَانَتْ لَهُمْ جَنَّاتُ الْفِرْدَوْسِ نُزُلًا ﴿١٠٧﴾ خَالِدِيْنَ فِيْهَا$$

41

لَا يَبْغُوْنَ عَنْهَا حِوَلًا ﴿١٠٨﴾

"Indeed, those who have believed and done righteous deeds-they will have the Gardens of Paradise as a lodging wherein they will abide eternally. They will not desire from it any transfer." (18:107-108)

In other words, a person will remain there forever and will never get bored or suffer from fatigue. Allāh ﷻ will cleanse a person of their sins so every person entering Jannah will be clean and pure.

At times, Allāh ﷻ may love a servant but their good deeds fall short. Therefore they are put through trials and tribulations. By placing a person through a difficulty, their position is elevated and they will be compensated with a greater reward.

The patience that the Sahābah ﷺ displayed in even the smallest of things renders us speechless and is something for us to ponder over. When the Prophet ﷺ was informed that Allāh ﷻ had alleviated the toothache suffered by Sayyidunā Abū Bakr ﷺ, he thought to himself that he had never been aware of his closest Companion's suffering despite it going on for seven years, Subhān-Allāh!

Just contemplate upon Sayyidunā Abū Bakr's ﷺ patience and endurance that not even his closest friend was aware of his seven years of intense pain because he had kept it to himself.

Another instance where Sayyidunā Abū Bakr ﷺ displayed extraordinary patience was in the cave where he remained in hiding from the polytheists. As the Prophet ﷺ lay soundly asleep in the lap of Sayyidunā Abū Bakr ؓ, a snake came out and stung him. He muffled the cries from the sheer intensity of the pain he felt but his eyes could not hold back the pain and the tears began to trickle down his cheeks and fell on the Prophet's ﷺ blessed face.

Immediately, the Prophet ﷺ was awoken and even when asked what had caused him to cry, he modestly replied that he had been bitten by a snake. The Prophet ﷺ placed his blessed saliva on the inflicted area and the pain and suffering immediately subsided.

Once a Walī (pious friend) of Allāh ﷻ fell and fractured his foot. Immediately he exclaimed, "Alhamdulillāh" (praise be to Allāh ﷻ)! Am I going to complain to Allāh ﷻ? Whatever He decrees, I am happy with. Everything good or bad is from Allāh ﷻ, O Allāh ﷻ whatever You do I am happy."

Even when our pious predecessors did not get what they asked for, they remained equally content in acknowledging the fact that Allāh ﷻ did not give them that particular thing because He had decreed something better for them. In other words, at times we may ask Allāh ﷻ for something that we think is good for us, but in reality it is something that will bring us misery. This is why Allāh ﷻ does not allow it for us in this life, but stores a reward for us in the Hereafter which will be far greater in excelling all our expectations.

Sayyidunā Sa'd Ibn Abī Waqqās ؓ was one of the Companions that the Prophet ﷺ was so pleased with, that he prayed to Allāh ﷻ that He accepts all his Du'ās. This is exactly what happened such that people would flock to him to request that he makes Du'ā for them.

Once he had visited Makkah Mukarramah to perform Hajj and people had flocked around him asking him to make Du'ā for them. Amongst them were those who were blind and when Sayyidunā Sa'd Ibn Abī Waqqās ؓ made Du'ā for them, their sight became restored. Upon this, many stood amazed and asked why he did not supplicate to Allāh ﷻ for himself as he had been struck with blindness during his latter days. He promptly replied that he was content with what Allāh ﷻ had destined for him to a far greater degree than what he desired for himself.

When a person has contentment upon *Taqdīr* (predestination), then Allāh ﷻ will forgive them for their sins and enter them into gardens beneath which rivers flow.

Types of Hypocrisy

After the verse in Sūrah Al-Fath which describes the rewards that the righteous will attain, Allāh ﷻ says:

$$\text{وَيُعَذِّبَ الْمُنَافِقِينَ وَالْمُنَافِقَاتِ وَالْمُشْرِكِينَ وَالْمُشْرِكَاتِ الظَّآنِّينَ بِاللهِ ظَنَّ السَّوْءِ ۚ عَلَيْهِمْ دَآئِرَةُ السَّوْءِ ۖ وَغَضِبَ اللهُ عَلَيْهِمْ وَلَعَنَهُمْ وَأَعَدَّ لَهُمْ جَهَنَّمَ ۖ وَسَآءَتْ مَصِيرًا}$$

"And (that) He may punish the hypocrite men and hypocrite women, and the polytheist men and polytheist women, those who assume about Allāh an assumption of evil nature. Upon them is a misfortune of evil nature and Allāh has become angry with them and has cursed them and prepared for them Hell and evil it is as the destination." (48:6)

This verse denotes a direct contrast to the original proposition put forward in the verse before. The Munāfiqūn (hypocrites) are the first group referred to here.

It is also important to note that there are two type of hypocrisy:

1. *Nifāq e Amalī*: hypocrisy in actions which will not take a person out of the fold of Islām and

2. *Nifāq e Itiqādī*: hypocrisy in the creed. This type of hypocrisy takes a person out of the fold of Islām. The people in this category only externally proclaim that they are believers but internally they do not have any faith. This is further explained in the following verse:

إِذَا جَآءَكَ الْمُنَافِقُونَ قَالُوا نَشْهَدُ إِنَّكَ لَرَسُولُ اللّهِ ۗ وَاللّهُ يَعْلَمُ إِنَّكَ لَرَسُولُهُ وَاللّهُ يَشْهَدُ إِنَّ الْمُنَافِقِينَ لَكَاذِبُونَ

"When the hypocrites come to you (O Muhammad) they say, 'We testify you are the Messenger of Allāh.' And Allāh knows that you are His Messenger and Allāh testifies that the hypocrites are liars." (63:1)

In another verse Allāh ﷺ says:

وَمِنَ النَّاسِ مَنْ يَّقُوْلُ اٰمَنَّا بِاللهِ وَبِالْيَوْمِ الْاٰخِرِ وَمَا هُمْ بِمُؤْمِنِيْنَ

"And of the people are some who say, ' We believe in Allāh and the Last Day,' but they are not believers." (2:8)

The disbelievers possessed evil thoughts regarding Allāh ﷺ and the believers. When the Muslims went into the battlefield, the hypocrites hoped that they would never return back. Allāh ﷺ explains that those who wish for this will go through disappointment and would be punished severely.

Sayyidunā Wāthila Ibnul Asqa ؓ reported that the Messenger of Allāh ﷺ said, "Do not rejoice over the misfortune of your brother lest Allāh ﷺ have mercy upon him and subject you to trials." (Tirmidhī)

Divine Help and Attributes of the Prophet ﷺ

وَلِلّٰهِ جُنُوْدُ السَّمَاوَاتِ وَالْأَرْضِ ۚ وَكَانَ اللّٰهُ عَزِيْزًا حَكِيْمًا

"And to Allāh belongs the soldiers of the heavens and the earth. And ever is Allāh Exalted in Might and Wise."(48:7)

If Allāh ﷺ willed, he could use the soldiers in the heavens to bring about the results. This was displayed in the battle of Badr when the angels were sent down to aid the believers to the extent that some of the believers witnessed the help of the angels on the battlefield.

When a person strives with their wealth and their life, there is no doubt that Allāh ﷻ will send down His divine assistance in aiding and helping them to achieve success.

The Prophet ﷺ was sent as a mercy for mankind, to guide people to the truth and the straight path with the divinely revealed message. The Prophet ﷺ will give witness that he conveyed the message to the people on the Day of Judgement:

$$ إِنَّا أَرْسَلْنَاكَ شَاهِدًا وَّمُبَشِّرًا وَّنَذِيْرًا $$

"Indeed, We have sent you as a witness and a bringer of good tidings and a warner." (48:8)

The Prophet ﷺ had many attributes and qualities. The three qualities that are mentioned in the above verse are:
1. **Shāhid** - a witness
2. **Mubashshir** - a bringer of good tidings
3. **Nazīr** - a warner

Shāhid: The Holy Prophet ﷺ himself will give witness that he not only conveyed the message, but the Prophets of all the other previous nations had a message that was delivered to them.

$$ وَكَذَٰلِكَ جَعَلْنَاكُمْ أُمَّةً وَّسَطًا لِّتَكُوْنُوْا شُهَدَآءَ عَلَى النَّاسِ وَيَكُوْنَ الرَّسُوْلُ عَلَيْكُمْ شَهِيْدًا $$

> **"And thus We have made you a just community that you will be witnesses over the people and the Messenger will be a witness over you." (2:143)**

On the Day of Judgement, the people of previous nations will try to deny and belie that any Prophet ﷺ was sent to them. The Ummah of Muhammad ﷺ will then be put forward. They will profess and give witness that the Prophets conveyed their message. The disbelievers will dispute how Ummah of Muhammad ﷺ could possibly stand witness when they were not present at that particular time? The Prophets will reply that Prophet Muhammad ﷺ was sent with the Holy Qur'ān which spoke of all the previous Messengers that had been sent to the different nations and how, not only did the people disbelieve, but many resorted to horrendous acts against the Prophets in an effort to prevent them from succeeding in their mission.

This is further elaborated in the following Hadīth where Imām Ahmad ﷺ and Imām Ibn Mājah ﷺ narrate that Sayyidunā Abū Sa'īd Al-Khudrī ﷺ said that the Messenger of Allāh ﷺ said, "A Prophet ﷺ will come on the Day of Resurrection accompanied by one man and a Prophet ﷺ will come accompanied by two men or more than that. Then his people will be called and it will be said to him, 'Did this one convey the message to you?' They will say, 'No.' It will be said to him, 'Did you convey the message to your people?' And he will say, 'Yes.' It will be said to him, 'Who will bear witness for you?' He will say, "Muhammad and his Ummah.' So Muhammad and his

Ummah will be called and it will be said to them, 'Did this one convey the message to his people?' They will say, 'Yes.' It will be said, 'How do you know that?' They will say, 'Our Prophet came to us and told us that the Messengers had conveyed the message.' That is the words of Allāh ﷻ, 'Thus We have made you a just (and the best) nation.' He said, 'Just so that you will be witnesses over mankind and the Messenger will be a witness over you."

At the time of Hajjatul Widā, on the historical day of Arafāt, the Prophet ﷺ addressed the crowd of pilgrims and asked, "Have I conveyed the Message?" The people responded, "You have completely fulfilled the Amānat. You have given Nasīhah (counselling) to the Ummah. The Prophet ﷺ then pointed his finger towards the heavens and said, "O Allāh ﷻ, be witness I have conveyed the Message."

Sayyidunā Ibn Mas'ūd ؓ reported that the Prophet ﷺ said to him, "Recite the Qur'ān to me." I said, "O Messenger of Allāh ﷺ! Shall I recite it to you when it was revealed to you?" He said, "I like to hear it from others." Then I began to recite Sūrah An-Nisā. When I reached the verse, " How will it be when We shall bring you as a witness against them?" (Having heard it) he said, "Enough! Enough!" When I looked at him, I found his eyes were overflowing with tears. (Bukhāri, Muslim)

How could our Prophet ﷺ not cry over the situation which the disbelievers will have to face on that day, remembering all the painstaking effort he undertook in a desperate attempt to bring them on the path of guidance, but to no avail? The Prophet ﷺ was sent as a mercy and it was his utmost desire to see that everybody was guided, but this was not to be.

Allāh ﷻ reminds the Prophet ﷺ that he could not guide whom he wished to, but it was up to Allāh ﷻ to open their hearts into accepting His call.

There will be those that even though they were given the message, they failed to adhere to it. Regarding them, it will be said on the Day of Judgement as mentioned in the Qur'ān:

وَقَالَ الرَّسُولُ يَٰرَبِّ إِنَّ قَوْمِي اتَّخَذُوا هَٰذَا الْقُرْآنَ مَهْجُورًا

"And the Messenger has said, "O my Lord, my people have taken this Qur'ān as (a thing) abandoned." (25:30)

We are all guilty of this to some degree as when the holy month of Ramadhān commences, the Qur'ān will be taken out and recited only to be put away when the month ends, until another entire year passes by waiting for the next Ramadhān to arrive when we will take it out again.

Allāh ﷻ says in the Qur'ān:

فَكَيْفَ إِذَا جِئْنَا مِن كُلِّ أُمَّةٍ بِشَهِيدٍ وَجِئْنَا بِكَ عَلَىٰ هَٰؤُلَاءِ شَهِيدًا

"So (how will it be) when We bring from every nation a witness, and We bring you (O Muhammad) against these (people) as a witness." (4:41)

The Prophet ﷺ is told in the Qur'ān:

وَذَكِّرْ فَإِنَّ الذِّكْرَى تَنْفَعُ الْمُؤْمِنِينَ

"And remind, for indeed the reminder benefits the believers." (51:55)

In another verse Allāh ﷺ reminds us:

وَجَاهِدُوا فِي اللهِ حَقَّ جِهَادِهِ ۚ هُوَ اجْتَبَاكُمْ وَمَا جَعَلَ عَلَيْكُمْ فِي الدِّينِ مِنْ حَرَجٍ ۚ مِلَّةَ
أَبِيكُمْ إِبْرَاهِيمَ ۚ هُوَ سَمَّاكُمُ الْمُسْلِمِينَ مِنْ قَبْلُ وَفِي هَٰذَا لِيَكُونَ الرَّسُولُ شَهِيدًا عَلَيْكُمْ
وَتَكُونُوا شُهَدَاءَ عَلَى النَّاسِ ۚ فَأَقِيمُوا الصَّلَاةَ وَآتُوا الزَّكَاةَ وَاعْتَصِمُوا بِاللهِ هُوَ مَوْلَاكُمْ ۖ
فَنِعْمَ الْمَوْلَى وَنِعْمَ النَّصِيرُ

"And strive for Allāh with the striving due to Him. He has chosen you and not placed upon you in the religion any difficulty. (It is) the religion of your father, Ibrāhīm. Allāh named you Muslims before (in former scriptures) and in this (revelation) that the Messenger may be a witness over you and you maybe witnesses over the people. So establish prayer and give Zakāh and hold fast to Allāh. He is your Protector, and excellent is the Protector and excellent is the Helper." (22:78)

The Prophet ﷺ will not only be made a witness of this Ummah but also a witness over the people of previous Ummahs (nations). In a Hadīth, it is stated that the good and bad deeds of all the people are put forward in front of the Prophet ﷺ every Mondays and Thursdays.

Mubashshir (a bringer of good tidings) which was the second attribute of the Holy Prophet ﷺ regarding which Sayyidunā Anas Ibn Mālik ؓ narrates that the Prophet ﷺ said, "Treat people with ease and do not be hard on them; give them glad tidings and do not make them run away (from Islām)." (Bukhāri, Muslim)

Moderation is the key to success. If we demand too much from the people, then this too will drive them away from the Dīn. Allāh ﷻ wants us to walk on the path of salvation and success. The love He has for His servants is greater than the love a mother has for her child.

Sayyidunā Umar ؓ reported: "Some prisoners of war were bought in front of the Prophet ﷺ and a woman was among them breastfeeding. Whenever she found a child among the prisoners, she would take it to her chest and nurse it. The Prophet ﷺ said to us, 'Do you think this woman could throw her child in the fire?' We said, 'No, not if she is able to stop it.' The Prophet ﷺ said, 'Allāh ﷻ is more Merciful to His servants than a mother is to her child.'" (Bukhāri)

Allāh ﷻ says in the Qur'ān:

مَا يَفْعَلُ اللّٰهُ بِعَذَابِكُمْ إِنْ شَكَرْتُمْ وَاٰمَنْتُمْ ۗ وَكَانَ اللّٰهُ شَاكِرًا عَلِيْمًا

"What would Allāh do with your punishment if you are grateful and believe? And ever is Allāh Appreciative and Know-

ing." (4:147)

In other words, Allāh ﷻ is urging us to consider what is there for Him to gain by punishing us, as this was not the reason why we were created in the first instance.

Nazīr (a warner) which was the third attribute of the Holy Prophet ﷺ. We were brought into existence to obey and worship our Creator, and this is why we were placed on this earth. By following and carrying out His commands, we will gain eternal pleasure but equally if we choose to disobey, we will have to face the consequences.

Many people may find this prospect daunting at times, but if we truly allow ourselves to envision the greater picture then a different image arises. When we go about our day-to-day occupation and pursuits, a familiar pattern arises. Despite what we are doing, we are always adhering within a framework of instructions. For example, if we are at work, we are abiding by the rules and regulations of the workplace and we are following a set practice. Whether we show a preference for it or dislike it, or simply put up with it is because we know that this is only a means to an end.

Similarly, there may be many things in life that we feel much inclined to do and other things that we wish to refrain from. Nonetheless and ultimately, the yardstick which we use to measure and deduce our thoughts and actions requires that to derive maximum benefit, we select the one that will give us the most significant outcome of positivity.

In identifying this we have to ensure that all the appropriate measures are taken. This may cause us some initial loss or suffering but we persevere because we know that the reward to be reaped at the end will far outweigh the hardship that we underwent and had to endure.

This is what Allāh ﷻ is explaining to us that even after all this, if a person chooses to do otherwise, they will have no one to blame except themselves. This is because of the prior warning about the consequences of misdeeds which justifies the punishment against them.

We have to maintain a balance. Just because certain criteria may go against our own preference and liking, if we recognise it to be the truth then we have to sacrifice our personal desires and attachments to be in conformity of what is expected of us. It is only then we will be able to move forward and attain real success both in this world and the next.

Patience and Gratitude

Allāh ﷻ says in the Qur'ān:

وَإِذْ تَأَذَّنَ رَبُّكُمْ لَئِن شَكَرْتُمْ لَأَزِيدَنَّكُمْ وَلَئِن كَفَرْتُمْ إِنَّ عَذَابِي لَشَدِيدٌ

"And (remember) when your Lord proclaimed, 'If you are grate-

ful, I will surely increase you (in favour), but if you deny, indeed My punishment is severe.'" (14:7)

How often are we grateful and express our gratitude to Allāh ﷻ for the countless and limitless blessings Allāh ﷻ has bestowed upon us. Our honourable Shaykh spoke of a man who was not only blind but had all his limbs missing. As he sat praising and expressing his gratitude to Allāh ﷻ, a man who was taken back by what he was witnessing approached the man and asked him what exactly he had to be grateful for. The man replied, "Should I not be grateful for the tongue Allāh ﷻ has given me so that I can do His Dhikr?" Subhān-Allāh!

The remarkable understanding and insight of our pious predecessors is an outstanding example we can all derive lessons from. Many of us may be blessed with so much but because of our pessimistic outlook on life, we fail to appreciate Allāh's ﷻ blessings.

As Muslims, we must convey the message of glad tidings given to those who believe and act according to the commands of Allāh ﷻ. There are many who are averse to saying anything positive and always feel a far greater need to highlight the punishment that will be inflicted if they fail to comply.

As humans, we are all composed of different temperaments and dispositions. Although at times a person may find themselves in sin, putting greater emphasis on the consequences of committing sins may add to further dampening a person's character, to the point that they become despondent and feel that all hope is lost.

Repentance

We are reminded many a times that as long as we feel remorseful and repentant for our sins, Allāh ﷻ will forgive us.

وَالَّذِيْنَ إِذَا فَعَلُوْا فَاحِشَةً أَوْ ظَلَمُوْٓا أَنْفُسَهُمْ ذَكَرُوا اللهَ فَاسْتَغْفَرُوْا لِذُنُوْبِهِمْ ۗ وَمَنْ يَّغْفِرُ الذُّنُوْبَ إِلَّا اللهُ وَلَمْ يُصِرُّوْا عَلٰى مَا فَعَلُوْا وَهُمْ يَعْلَمُوْنَ ١٣٥﴿ أُولٰۤئِكَ جَزَآؤُهُمْ مَّغْفِرَةٌ مِّنْ رَّبِّهِمْ وَجَنّٰتٌ تَجْرِيْ مِنْ تَحْتِهَا الْأَنْهٰرُ خٰلِدِيْنَ فِيْهَا ۗ وَنِعْمَ أَجْرُ الْعٰمِلِيْنَ ١٣٦﴿

"And those who when they commit an immorality or wrong themselves (by transgression), remember Allāh and seek forgiveness for their sins and who can forgive sins except Allāh? And (who) do not persist in what they have done while they know. For those their reward is forgiveness from their Lord and gardens beneath which rivers flow (in Paradise), wherein they will abide eternally, and excellent is the reward of the (righteous) workers." (3:135-136)

It is in the nature of man that he will err and commit sin, but what will elevate and purify a person from sin is when a person turns to Allāh ﷻ with a sincere repentance seeking forgiveness.

How Merciful Allāh ﷻ is! Even if the person falls back into committing the same sin and turns to Allāh ﷻ seeking His forgiveness, He will forgive him despite his re-offending.

In the Dunya, if we commit a mistake, more often than not, we will immediately be taken to task and we will have to bear the consequences of our actions. For repeat offences, the repercussions will be far greater. Yet Allāh ﷻ in His limitless mercy, does not punish us immediately but gives us a whole lifetime of opportunity to amend and rectify our conduct. Even after all this time of chance and opportunity someone neglected to rectify themselves, then they have no one to blame but themselves. We must strive and act now while we still have the chance because we do not know when our time will be cut short.

On the authority of Sayyidunā Sufyān Ibn Abdullāh ؓ who said, "O Messenger of Allāh ﷺ, tell me something about Islām which l do not need to ask anyone after you.' He said, 'Say, I believe in Allāh ﷻ and then be steadfast.'" (Muslim)

This Hadīth of our beloved Prophet ﷺ gives very concise and comprehensive advice on how a person can find true happiness and success. After having proclaimed belief in the oneness of Allāh ﷻ, we need to be dutifully firm and remain unwavering in the devotion and commitment to one's faith.

This is because by declaring our faith in Allāh ﷻ and His Messenger ﷺ, we become obligated to fulfil the requirements of belief. Allāh ﷻ says:

لِتُؤْمِنُوا بِاللّهِ وَرَسُوْلِهِ وَتُعَزِّرُوْهُ وَتُوَقِّرُوْهُ وَتُسَبِّحُوْهُ بُكْرَةً وَّأَصِيْلًا

"That you (people) may believe in Allāh and His Messenger and honour him and respect the Prophet and exalt Allāh morning and afternoon." (48:9)

The Arabic word used in this verse is *'Watu'azzirū'* which means to honour, respect and show reverence. In this context, the pronoun that has been used denotes both showing respect to Allāh ﷻ and His Messenger ﷺ. Displaying respect to Allāh ﷻ can take the form of assisting His Dīn. A person fulfils whatever Allāh ﷻ has ordered and does not violate His commands.

The Arabic word that follows is *'Watuwaqqirū'* which means to respect a person in the highest regard in recognition of their virtues and qualities.

Reverence for the Dīn (Religion)

Sayyidunā Tamīm Ad-Dāri ؓ said, "The Prophet ﷺ said, (three times), 'The Religion is Nasīhah (sincerity and sincere advice).' We said, 'To whom?' He said, 'To Allāh, His Book, His Messenger and to the leaders of the Muslims and the general people.'" (Muslim)

To show reverence and respect for the Dīn of Allāh ﷻ is to obey Allāh ﷻ in performing and discharging one's duties. In following the Prophet ﷺ, it is in assisting him; in following his Sunnah. The Sa-

58

hābah 🙵 are the benchmark and our prime role models for following the Sunnah as there are countless incidents where the practically demonstrated this.

Sincerity to the leaders means obeying and assisting them. For example, sincerity to the Sahābah 🙵 meant following them and spreading the Dīn of Islām; in striving in the path of Allāh 🙵.

In Sūrah Al-Hujurāt, regarding the disrespectful and discourteous mannerism displayed towards the Prophet 🙵, Allāh 🙵 says:

إِنَّ الَّذِيْنَ يُنَادُوْنَكَ مِنْ وَّرَآءِ الْحُجُرَاتِ اَكْثَرُهُمْ لَا يَعْقِلُوْنَ

"Indeed, those who call you (O Muhammad) from behind the chambers most of them do not use reason. (49:4)

Before the revelation of the verses, many people would address the Prophet 🙵 and speak to him as they would converse amongst one another. This was a display of great ignorance of his superior nobility and higher-ranking status. Respect should be given according to people of all ages and levels and according to their status.

The Prophet 🙵 said, "He is not of us who does not have mercy on young children nor honour the elderly." (Tirmidhī)

Sayyidunā Abū Bakr ⬥ and his Love for the Prophet ⬥

Our Shaykh spoke about the great love, honour and respect Sayyidunā Abū Bakr ⬥ had for the Prophet ⬥ and his ability to apply and demonstrate these qualities when in need. At the time when the Prophet ⬥ migrated to Madīnah Munawwarah, as they entered the city, the people came rushing to greet them. Despite Sayyidunā Abū Bakr ⬥ being two years younger than the Prophet ⬥, his appearance gave the impression that he was of senior age. This led to people mistaking him to be the Prophet ⬥ and as a result, they wished to shake his hand.

Sayyidunā Abū Bakr ⬥ seeing that the Prophet ⬥ was tired after the long journey, continued shaking the hands of all the people wishing not to inconvenience him. It was only when Sayyidunā Abū Bakr ⬥ shielded the Prophet ⬥ against the rays of the piercing sun that the people recognised the identity of the Prophet ⬥.

The sheer lack of manners and common courtesy today is evident in our society with social media demonstrating this in alarming proportions. Even respect and regard when it comes to seniors or elders is not reserved or expressed for them. Where once respect, esteem and honour could be earned through serving the people through effort and endeavour, now it is bought by the wealthy, powerful and elite. We must return it to its true origins in recognising its true quality and worth. Only then can we wish to be successful in instilling this virtue back into our society.

In Sahīh Al-Bukhāri there is a Hadīth narrated by Sayyidunā Sahl Ibn Sa'd ؓ where he mentions that once the Prophet ﷺ had gone out to arbitrate a dispute. The time for prayer had arrived but the Prophet ﷺ had not returned. Upon the request of Sayyidunā Bilāl ؓ, Sayyidunā Abū Bakr ؓ began to lead the prayer. The Prophet ﷺ arrived moments later and joined the first row and beckoned Sayyidunā Abū Bakr ؓ with his hand to continue leading the prayer. Sayyidunā Abū Bakr ؓ raised his hands and praised Allāh ﷻ and then retreated till he came in the (first) row. The Prophet ﷺ moved forward and lead the prayer. After the Prophet ﷺ finished the prayer, he asked Sayyidunā Abū Bakr ؓ, "O Abū Bakr! What prevented you from leading the people in the prayer when I beckoned to you (to continue)?" Sayyidunā Abū Bakr ؓ replied, "It did not befit the son of Abū Quhāfa to lead the prayer in front of the Prophet ﷺ."

Sayyidunā Abū Bakr ؓ did not disobey the Prophet's ﷺ order, but understood and interpreted his instructions according to the situation that had arisen. Owing to the modest and humble nature of our beloved Prophet ﷺ, seeing that the prayer had already commenced, He chose to respectfully join the prayer from behind.

Sayyidunā Abū Bakr ؓ, in recognising the great honour and respect given to him by our beloved Prophet ﷺ repaid this appreciation by realising that he was not the rightful person befitting this honour of leading the prayer while the Prophet ﷺ was alive and present amongst them. This would have only further increased Sayyidunā Abū Bakr's ؓ standing in the eyes of the Prophet ﷺ for his matchless virtues and qualities of mannerism and decorum, displayed through his behaviour in the Prophet's ﷺ noble presence.

We are left with awe and amazement at the sheer level of love the Sahābah ؓ had for the Prophet ﷺ who left no stone unturned in showing the greatest level of love, respect and obedience to him.

The Prophet ﷺ did not limit showing respect and courtesy to people alone. Even animals were given the right to be treated with love and care. He taught people that animals must not be overburdened and overworked. The animals in the Arabian peninsula roamed around openly and freely without the threat of suffering from torture and cruelty. This is because they were under protection from over 1300 years before the first Animals Rights group which was established in the United States by Henry Bergh in April 1866.

Glorify your Lord

The words that follow in the verse that comes after are:

$$وَتُسَبِّحُوهُ بُكْرَةً وَأَصِيلًا$$

"And exalt Allāh morning and afternoon." (48:9)

There are various meanings given to this verse by the commentators of the Holy Qur'ān. One interpretation is that it refers to the daily Salāh. Another explanation of this verse is to praise and glorify Allāh

. It is mentioned in Bukhāri and Muslim that Sayyidunā Abū Hurairah reported, "He who utters 'Subhān-Allāhi wa bi-hamdihī' (Allāh is free from imperfection and His is the Praise), one hundred times a day, his sins will be obliterated even if they are equal to the foam of the ocean."

There are so many Tasbīhāt that we can engage in reciting which are light on the tongue and heavy on the scales, i.e. these deeds are very easy to perform and carry out but we have an enormous reward.

In another Hadīth the Prophet said, "Is anyone of you incapable of earning a thousand Hasanah (rewards) a day?" Someone from the gathering asked, "How can anybody from us earn a thousand Hasanah?" The Prophet said, "Glorify Allāh one hundred times a day by saying, 'Subhān-Allāh' and good deeds will be written for you or a thousand sins will be wiped away." (Muslim)

The verse is not only restricted to praising and glorifying Allāh in the morning and evening but engaging in dhikr continuously. The purpose of our existence is to worship our creator just as Allāh says:

$$وَمَا خَلَقْتُ الْجِنَّ وَالْإِنْسَ إِلَّا لِيَعْبُدُونِ$$
"And I did not create the jinn and mankind except to worship Me." (51:56)

Even when a person enters Paradise, although they will not feel disappointment in the slightest bit, they will still have one regret. The Prophet ﷺ said, *"The people of Paradise will not have any regrets except for those moments in which they were not engaged in the dhikr of Allāh ﷻ."*

Obedience to the Prophet ﷺ

إِنَّ الَّذِينَ يُبَايِعُوْنَكَ إِنَّمَا يُبَايِعُوْنَ اللهَ يَدُ اللهِ فَوْقَ أَيْدِيْهِمْ ۚ فَمَنْ نَكَثَ فَإِنَّمَا يَنْكُثُ عَلَى نَفْسِهٖ ۖ وَمَنْ أَوْفٰى بِمَا عَاهَدَ عَلَيْهُ اللهَ فَسَيُؤْتِيْهِ أَجْرًا عَظِيْمًا

"Indeed, those who pledge allegiance to you (O Muhammad), they are actually pledging allegiance to Allāh. The hand of Allāh is over their hands. So he who breaks his word, only breaks it to the detriment of himself. And he who fulfils that which he has promised Allāh, He will give him a great reward." (48:10)

"The hand of Allāh ﷻ is over their hands" in this verse refers to Allāh's ﷻ help and assistance surrounding and shielding the believers. Also, the denotation extends to that of Allāh ﷻ being pleased with them.

There were 1400 Sahābah ؓ who swore allegiance to the Prophet ﷺ that they would fight until their last breath, to what they believed would be to avenge the death of Sayyidunā Uthmān ؓ. This is because rumours were circulating that there had been foul play whilst he had been detained by the polytheists of Makkah Mukarramah. By obeying the Prophet ﷺ and taking the pledge, the Sahābah ؓ were

64

making the pledge with Allāh ﷻ.

After the polytheists heard about the determination of the Sahābah ؓ in pledging to fight until death, they were cast with fear in their hearts and released Sayyidunā Uthmān ؓ immediately.

Types of Allegiance

There are different levels of allegiance as follows:
1. *Bay'at alal Islām* - the allegiance a person takes when they enter into Islām.
2. *Bay'at lil Khilāfa* - the pledge of allegiance to the Khalīfah (leader) in committing to obey them in every legal matter.
3. *Bay'at lil Amalis Sālih* - the oath of allegiance taken for carrying out good deeds. This was also practised during the Prophet's ﷺ time.

Sayyidunā Jarīr Ibn Abdullāh ؓ said, "I gave the pledge of allegiance to the Prophet ﷺ for offering prayer perfectly, giving Zakāt and giving good advice to every Muslim." He went to great length to uphold this pledge.

Once he sent his servant to buy a horse for him. The servant purchased the horse for 400 Dirhams and returned back home with it. Sayyidunā Jarīr Ibn Abdullāh ؓ went back to the market place with the horse and upon finding the seller he insisted that he wanted to renegotiate the purchase price of the horse. The seller agreed and Sayyidunā Jarīr Ibn Abdullāh ﷺ steadily increase the price of the horse until he settled at 800 Dirhams, much to the utter amazement of the seller. This is because he was already content with receiving the 400 Dirhams from the original transaction. Sayyidunā Jarīr Ibn Abdullāh ﷺ explained to the seller that he had underestimated the price of the horse. Therefore he wanted to pay him the correct market value of it which was in accordance with the allegiance he had sworn to the Prophet ﷺ.

In this case, the seller stood to lose out on profit owing to the fact that he was not familiar with the actual value of the horse. Therefore, despite the fact that Sayyidunā Jarīr Ibn Abdullāh ﷺ ended up paying double the amount of what he had originally paid, he wished to give the value that the horse was truly worth.

This was the level of piety and Taqwa they had in their hearts. The true sense of goodwill in showing their compassion and benevolence to their Muslim brother. Their level of care and concern resulted in scrutinising and inspecting every angle before settling a matter because of the level of seriousness they attached to their commitments. This is a far cry to the behaviour we witness today. Let alone paying the right amount for a purchase, many of us would try to unlawfully take the property given half a chance.

Also regarding the matter of charging the correct price; nowadays it is a common practice for people to overcharge others in selling even basic things such as food and other fundamental essentials.

Our own beloved Shaykh narrated an incident where he purchased an exotic cocktail for his wife displayed in a shop picture. Upon arriving home he discovered that he had been given some pieces of apples floating around in a fruit cocktail which could only be likened to some rotten pieces of fruit. The seller had been dishonest in his transaction.

Another incident which took place in a similar area was when our Shaykh had got into a taxi only to realise that they were trying to charge him ten times the amount of the average cost of a journey of similar length. The driver; thinking that he was a foreigner to the country tried to take advantage of his naivety of being in what he thought was unfamiliar land until our Shaykh exposed his greed.

Sayyidunā Zubair Ibn Awwām ﷺ was a Companion whom many would entrust their wealth and possession with. He was extremely adamant of ensuring that whatever was entrusted with him should be paid back in full without the risk of any loss. Therefore, he would take it upon himself to look after people's wealth as a Qardh (loan) and not as an Amānat (trust).

There is a difference between a Qardh and an Amānat from a jurisprudence point of view. If a person agreed to look after someone's wealth as an Amānat and thereafter despite their best efforts to protect it, it was lost or stolen, then they are dissolved of any responsibility to pay it back. However, if a person was to lose a Qardh, they will still be obliged to return the wealth. Now we can understand the extent that Sayyidunā Zubair Ibn Awwām ﷺ had gone to for the benefit of others.

Before Sayyidunā Zubair Ibn Awwām ﷺ passed away, his debts amounted to 2.2 million Dirhams. In the Battle of Jamal (Camel), he called out to his son saying that he felt that maybe he would be martyred and should this be the outcome then his debt should be settled. He advised his son that if at anytime he was faced with difficulty in repaying off the debt, he should refer to his Mawlā (Protector). His son enquired who this was and Sayyidunā Zubair Ibn Awām ﷺ replied, "Allāh ﷻ."

His goods and assets comprised of vast amounts of estates and properties. A staggering 1.6 million Dirhams alone was obtained upon the sale of a piece of land. After settling his debts, each one of his four wives inherited 1.2 million Dirhams. This only accounted for one-eighth of the wealth that remained, so one could only imagine how much wealth he possessed. Allāh ﷻ blessed his wealth with so much Barakah that he was a multi-millionaire of his time.

Spiritual Rectification

The Prophet ﷺ was the purifier, cleanser and remover of spiritual maladies from the Sahābah ﷺ. He was the spiritual guide that led the way in advising and counselling them to relieve them of their spiritual ailments and delivered them into the strong foothold of spiritual refinement, whereby they derived an elevated state of being in their attachment and bond with Allāh ﷻ.

The people of Tazkiyah work on rectifying the heart. Taking *Bay'ah* is Sunnah, but the need to purify one's heart is a Fardh (compulsory). A person who does not take Bay'ah will find it considerably difficult, if not impossible to rectify their heart.

Just as a person cannot become a doctor through the study of medicine books alone and needs a person to teach and equip them with the skills, similarly, a person cannot spiritually rectify themselves without a mentor. A spiritual guide provides and facilitates the efficiency and expertise of cleansing and purifying a person's heart spiritually.

For those who fulfil the promise pledged in the Bay'ah, for them is an excellent reward from Allāh ﷻ as mentioned in verse 10 of Sūrah Al-Fath.

Sayyidunā Abū Hurairah ؓ reported that the Prophet ﷺ said, " A man is upon the religion of his best friend, so let one of you look at whom he befriends." (Abū Dāwūd)

A pious predecessor said, "Stay in the company of the pious until you become like them." The Prophet ﷺ was reportedly asked, "Which of our Companions is best?" He replied: "One whose appearance reminds you of Allāh ﷻ and whose speech increases you in knowledge and whose actions reminds you of the Hereafter."

The Hypocrites

The hypocrites had no intention of staying in the company of the believers or assisting them in any matter and seized every opportunity in staying afar. Yet, they covered up their tracks in a pretentious act of being sincere. However, Allāh ﷻ discloses their true intentions:

سَيَقُولُ لَكَ الْمُخَلَّفُونَ مِنَ الْأَعْرَابِ شَغَلَتْنَا أَمْوَالُنَا وَأَهْلُونَا فَاسْتَغْفِرْ لَنَا ۚ يَقُولُونَ بِأَلْسِنَتِهِم مَّا لَيْسَ فِي قُلُوبِهِمْ ۚ قُلْ فَمَن يَمْلِكُ لَكُم مِّنَ اللَّهِ شَيْئًا إِنْ أَرَادَ بِكُمْ ضَرًّا أَوْ أَرَادَ بِكُمْ نَفْعًا ۚ بَلْ كَانَ اللَّهُ بِمَا تَعْمَلُونَ خَبِيرًا

"Those who remained of the Bedouins will say to you, 'Our properties and our families occupied us, so ask forgiveness for us.' They say with their tongues what is not within their hearts. Say, 'Then who could prevent Allāh at all if He intended for you harm or intended for you benefit? Rather, ever is Allāh with what you do, Acquainted.'" (48:11)

Due to the empathy and compassion of the Prophet ﷺ, he would always overlook their faults and forgive them. The hypocrites on the other hand hid their sinister motives and would be the first to present their excuses one after the other.

At the time of the battle of Khandaq (Battle of the Trench) they complained to the Prophet ﷺ that their houses were exposed and they feared that their womenfolk would be attacked. Allāh ﷻ exposes their deceitful behaviour in the following verse:

70

وَإِذْ قَالَت طَّآئِفَةٌ مِّنْهُمْ يَـٰٓأَهْلَ يَثْرِبَ لَا مُقَامَ لَكُمْ فَٱرْجِعُوا۟ ۚ وَيَسْتَـٔذِنُ فَرِيقٌ مِّنْهُمُ ٱلنَّبِىَّ

يَقُولُونَ إِنَّ بُيُوتَنَا عَوْرَةٌ وَمَا هِىَ بِعَوْرَةٍ ۖ إِن يُرِيدُونَ إِلَّا فِرَارًا

"And when a faction of them said, 'O people of Yathrib, there is
no stability for you (here), so return (home).'" And a party of
them asked permission of the Prophet, saying, 'Indeed, our
houses are unprotected,' while they were not exposed. They did
not intend except to flee." (33:13)

Our situation today also leaves us not far behind. For many of us,
our wealth and our children become a trial which prevents us from
going forward in obeying Allāh ﷻ for fear of incurring loss to our
wealth and our lives. Allāh ﷻ says:

إِنَّمَآ أَمْوَٰلُكُمْ وَأَوْلَـٰدُكُمْ فِتْنَةٌ ۚ وَٱللَّهُ عِندَهُۥٓ أَجْرٌ عَظِيمٌ

"Your wealth and your children are but a trial and Allāh has with
Him a great reward." (64:15)

It was narrated from Sayyidunā Ya'lā Al-Āmir ؓ that he said: "Hasan
and Husain came running to the Prophet ﷺ and he embraced them
and said, "Children make a man a miser or a coward." (Ibn Mājah)

In other words, a person becomes a miser in spending fearing the
decline in his wealth. They became overpowered by cowardliness
from fighting in the cause of Allāh ﷻ afraid that there will be no one
to look after their children if they are killed. Even fulfilling a person's
obligation become filled with fear.

After the incident that took place in 2015 where some people lost their lives whilst performing Hajj (pilgrimage), the following year as the time for Hajj grew close, there were many people who disagreed with going. They voiced their protests claiming that they feared they too would meet the same fate of those who lost their lives.

If our worldly commitments are stopping us from fulfilling our obligatory duties, then indeed we are heading for the greatest loss imaginable.

The Sahābah ﷺ displayed the true embodiment of obedience and submission when it came to following Allāh ﷺ and the Prophet's ﷺ commands. Allāh ﷺ says regarding this:

رِجَالٌ لَّا تُلْهِيهِمْ تِجَارَةٌ وَّلَا بَيْعٌ عَن ذِكْرِ اللهِ وَإِقَامِ الصَّلوٰةِ وَإِيتَآءِ الزَّكوٰةِ ۙ يَخَافُونَ يَوْمًا تَتَقَلَّبُ فِيهِ الْقُلُوبُ وَالْأَبْصَارُ

"(Are) men whom neither commerce nor sale distracts from the remembrance of Allāh and performance of prayer and giving of Zakāt. They fear a day in which the hearts and eyes will (fearfully) turn about." (24:37)

We should be fearful of a day when all will be laid out bare. We shall see the reality with our eyes but it will be too late to change anything as explained in the following verse:

لَقَدْ كُنتَ فِي غَفْلَةٍ مِّنْ هٰذَا فَكَشَفْنَا عَنكَ غِطَآءَكَ فَبَصَرُكَ الْيَوْمَ حَدِيدٌ

"(It will be said), 'You were certainly in unmindfulness of this and We have removed from you your cover, so your sight this day is sharp." (50:22)

The hypocrites thought that they were fooling the Prophet ﷺ with their feeble excuses, but the only ones they were beguiling were themselves.

Signs of Hypocrisy

Regarding the hypocrites Allāh ﷻ says:

يُخَادِعُونَ اللهَ وَالَّذِينَ اٰمَنُوْا وَمَا يَخْدَعُوْنَ إِلَّا أَنْفُسَهُمْ وَمَا يَشْعُرُوْنَ

"They (think to) deceive Allāh and those who believe, but they deceive not except themselves and perceive (it) not." (2:9)

Sayyidunā Abū Hurairah ؓ reported that the Messenger of Allāh ﷺ said, "The signs of a hypocrite are three, even if he fasts and prays and claims to be a Muslim: When he speaks he lies, when he gives a promise he breaks it and when he is trusted he is treacherous." (Bukhārī)

This is further explained in the following verse:

وَمِنَ النَّاسِ مَنْ يَّقُوْلُ اٰمَنَّا بِاللهِ وَبِالْيَوْمِ الْاٰخِرِ وَمَا هُمْ بِمُؤْمِنِيْنَ

"And of the people are some who say, 'We believe in Allāh and the Last Day,' but they are not believers." (2:8)

In another verse revealing the ploy of the hypocrites, Allāh ﷺ says:

إِذَا جَآءَكَ الْمُنَافِقُونَ قَالُوا نَشْهَدُ إِنَّكَ لَرَسُولُ اللّٰهِ ۗ وَاللّٰهُ يَعْلَمُ إِنَّكَ لَرَسُولُهُ ۚ وَاللّٰهُ يَشْهَدُ إِنَّ الْمُنَافِقِينَ لَكَاذِبُونَ

"When the hypocrites come to you (O Muhammad) they say, 'We testify that you are the Messenger of Allāh.' And Allāh knows that you are His Messenger and Allāh testifies that the hypocrites are liars." (63:1)

The hypocrites will find themselves burning in the lowest depths of Hellfire as mentioned in the following verse:

إِنَّ الْمُنَافِقِينَ فِي الدَّرْكِ الْأَسْفَلِ مِنَ النَّارِ وَلَنْ تَجِدَ لَهُمْ نَصِيرًا

"Indeed, the hypocrites will be in the lowest depths of the Fire- and never will you find for them a helper." (4:145)

In a Hadīth, it is related regarding the hypocrites: "Whoever had two faces in the worldly life, will have two tongues of fire on the Day of Resurrection." (Abū Dāwūd)

Allāh ﷺ says:

بَلْ ظَنَنْتُمْ أَنْ لَنْ يَنْقَلِبَ الرَّسُولُ وَالْمُؤْمِنُونَ إِلَى أَهْلِيهِمْ أَبَدًا وَزُيِّنَ ذٰلِكَ فِي قُلُوبِكُمْ

وَظَنَنتُم ظَنَّ السَّوءِ وَكُنتُم قَومًا بُورًا

"But you thought that the Messenger and the believers would
never return to their families, ever, and that was made pleasing
in your hearts. And you assumed an assumption of evil and became ruined people." (48:12)

If a death has been decreed for a person, even if they refuse to go out
to the battlefield, they will still meet their end. Allāh ﷻ says:

يَقُولُونَ لَو كَانَ لَنَا مِنَ الأَمرِ شَيءٌ مَّا قُتِلنَا هَٰهُنَا ۗ قُل لَّو كُنتُم فِي بُيُوتِكُم لَبَرَزَ الَّذِينَ كُتِبَ
عَلَيهِمُ القَتلُ إِلَىٰ مَضَاجِعِهِم

"They say, 'If there was anything we could have done in the
matter, some of us might have not been killed right here. Say,
'Even if you had been inside your homes, those decreed to be
killed would have come out to their deathbeds.'" (3:154)

The hypocrites thought that the Prophet ﷺ would surely meet his
end at the battlefield. To this, Allāh ﷻ revealed the following verse:

وَمَا جَعَلنَا لِبَشَرٍ مِّن قَبلِكَ الخُلدَ ۖ أَفَإِن مِّتَّ فَهُمُ الخَالِدُونَ

"And We did not grant to any man before you eternity (on
earth), so if you die, would they be eternal?" (21:34)

Even when the Prophet's ﷺ infant son passed away, the disbelievers
rejoiced thinking that the propagation of his message would be ter-
minated as he had no male offspring to continue his legacy. Allāh ﷻ

responds to them by saying:

إِنَّآ أَعْطَيْنَٰكَ ٱلْكَوْثَرَ ﴿١﴾ فَصَلِّ لِرَبِّكَ وَٱنْحَرْ ﴿٢﴾ إِنَّ شَانِئَكَ هُوَ ٱلْأَبْتَرُ ﴿٣﴾

**"(O Prophet) surely We have given to you Al-Kawthar. So, offer
Salāh (prayer) to your Lord and sacrifice. Indeed, your enemy is
the one cut off." (108:1-3)**

In other words, those in opposition will be the ones left without a
genealogy and will be forgotten about.

The hypocrites thought that with the Prophet's ﷺ demise in the
battlefield, leadership would return into their hands. Allāh ﷻ reminds us that power and sovereignty belong to Him and it is He
Who decides who should inherit these attributes and qualities.

وَلِلَّهِ مُلْكُ ٱلسَّمَٰوَٰتِ وَٱلْأَرْضِ يَغْفِرُ لِمَن يَشَآءُ وَيُعَذِّبُ مَن يَشَآءُ وَكَانَ ٱللَّهُ غَفُورًا رَّحِيمًا

**"And to Allāh belongs the dominion of the heavens and the
earth. He forgives whom He wills and punishes whom He wills.
And ever is Allāh Forgiving and Merciful." (48:14)**

Further to this Allāh ﷻ says regarding the hypocrites:

يَقُولُونَ لَئِن رَّجَعْنَآ إِلَى ٱلْمَدِينَةِ لَيُخْرِجَنَّ ٱلْأَعَزُّ مِنْهَا ٱلْأَذَلَّ وَلِلَّهِ ٱلْعِزَّةُ وَلِرَسُولِهِ
وَلِلْمُؤْمِنِينَ وَلَٰكِنَّ ٱلْمُنَافِقِينَ لَا يَعْلَمُونَ

**"They say, 'If we return to Madīnah, the more honoured (for
power) will surely expel therefrom the more humble.' And to**

Allāh belongs (all) honour and to His Messenger and to the believers, but the hypocrites do not know." (63:8)

Participation in Khybar

Those who did not participate in the treaty of Hudaybiyah were prevented from accompanying the Prophet ﷺ in the battle of Khybar. Allāh ﷻ says:

سَيَقُولُ الْمُخَلَّفُونَ إِذَا انْطَلَقْتُمْ إِلَى مَغَانِمَ لِتَأْخُذُوهَا ذَرُونَا نَتَّبِعْكُمْ ۚ يُرِيدُونَ أَن يُبَدِّلُوا كَلَٰمَ اللَّهِ ۚ قُل لَّن تَتَّبِعُونَا كَذَٰلِكُمْ قَالَ اللَّهُ مِن قَبْلُ ۚ فَسَيَقُولُونَ بَلْ تَحْسُدُونَنَا ۚ بَلْ كَانُوا لَا يَفْقَهُونَ إِلَّا قَلِيلًا

"Those who lagged behind will say when you depart to collect the gains, 'Let us follow you.' They want to change the Word of Allāh. Say, 'You will not follow us; Allāh has said so before.' Then they will say, 'But you are jealous of us.' In fact, they understand only a little." (48:15)

The hypocrites on seeing the success of the Muslims in Hudaybiyah felt that the Jews who resided in Khybar would be no match for the Muslims. Hence they were eager to join knowing that the conquest of Khybar would provide them with ample amount of booty and wealth.

The Prophet ﷺ received the revelation that only those who participated in the battle would be allowed to march forth. This lead to a turning point in the great amassment of booty and wealth, the likes of which the newly formed community of Muslims needed and welcomed after suffering from great need and destitution.

Before this campaign, many had fled their homes from Makkah Mukarramah to start a life in Madīnah Munawwarah and found themselves destitute of the physical comforts they had left behind. The conquest of Khybar opened the gates to newly acquired wealth which the new community were blessed with.

The hypocrites felt that they too had a right to acquire gains from the conquest of Khybar and felt the Muslims were envious. At the same time they were utterly oblivious to the fact that the believers had risked their own lives in obedience to the Prophet ﷺ and therefore fully deserved any measurable rewards that followed.

On the other hand, the true hypocrites had only sown the seeds of rebellion in an attempt to prevent the people from joining the Prophet ﷺ, hoping that this would lead him to perish in the battle.

They had plotted and planned, and now they thought when victory was imminent and the spoils of war were to be drawn forth; they too would be entitled to an equal share. How deluded they had become and Allāh ﷻ reveals their delusion by cutting short their evil ploy by exposing them in preventing them from marching forth, conveying the message that you only get to reap the fruits of what you sow.

Types of Revelation

Revelation (Wahī) is of two types:
1. **Wahī-e-Matlū:** Revelation which Allāh ﷻ has transmitted in His own words and speech, i.e. the Qur'ān.
2. **Wahī-e-Ghair Matlū:** Revelation that Allāh ﷻ transpired and projected in the heart of the Prophet ﷺ through Hadīth. The Prophet ﷺ revealed these orders to the people in his own words. In relation to this, Allāh ﷻ says:

$$﴿٥﴾ عَلَّمَهُ شَدِيْدُ الْقُوٰى ﴿٤﴾ إِنْ هُوَ إِلَّا وَحْيٌ يُّوْحٰى ﴿٣﴾ وَمَا يَنْطِقُ عَنِ الْهَوٰى$$

"Nor does he speak from (his own) inclination. It is not but a revelation revealed, taught to him by one intense in strength." (53:3-5)

The revelation the Prophet ﷺ received regarding Khybar was of the latter type. He was guided through divine intervention and not through his whims and desires, hence directing his followers from the path of darkness into the path of light and truth.

We also have a Mutawātir Hadīth which is a category of traditions or sayings of the Prophet ﷺ narrated by such a large number of people in a manner that the narrators are unanimous in reporting it without any disparity or disagreement.

Examples of Mutawātir practices are the five daily prayers, fasting in the holy month of Ramadhān, giving Zakāt at a stipulated amount, performing the Hajj and the recitation of the Holy Qur'ān. A Muta-wātir Hadīth becomes obligatory to practice and follow.

A Military Encounter

قُلْ لِلْمُخَلَّفِينَ مِنَ الْأَعْرَابِ سَتُدْعَوْنَ إِلَى قَوْمٍ أُولِي بَأْسٍ شَدِيدٍ تُقَاتِلُونَهُمْ أَوْ يُسْلِمُونَ ۚ فَإِن تُطِيعُوا يُؤْتِكُمُ اللهُ أَجْرًا حَسَنًا ۖ وَإِن تَتَوَلَّوْا كَمَا تَوَلَّيْتُم مِّن قَبْلُ يُعَذِّبْكُمْ عَذَابًا أَلِيمًا

"Say to those who remained behind of the Bedouin, 'You will be called to (face) people of great military might; you may fight them or they will submit. So if you obey, Allāh will give you a good reward; if you turn away as you turned away before, He will punish you with a painful punishment." (48:16)

Scholars differed as to who the people being referred to here are. Although at first sight, it appears to be addressing the Bedouins, they were not allowed to accompany the Prophet ﷺ on the expedition of Khybar. Also during the conquest of Makkah Mukarramah and during the expedition of Hunain and Tabūk, the Bedouins did not participate. In these expeditions, no real battle or fighting took place.

When the Romans heard about the army of 30,000 strong Muslims marching forth in the expedition of Tabūk, they decided that it would be in their best interest not to attack. They were instilled by the awe and the fear of the Muslims.

The Battle of Banū Hanīfah in Al-Yamāmah against Musaylamah Kazzāb is seen by many scholars to fit the description given by Allāh ﷻ in the above verse which speaks about a military encounter. At that moment in time, the situation of the Muslims was very volatile and strained.

After the Prophet's ﷺ demise, on the one hand there were those who refused to pay Zakāt and on the other hand was a man who was claiming Prophethood and had converted thousands from Banū Hanīfah.

In fact, the false claim to Prophethood had been pursued by Musaylamah Kazzāb just before the Prophet ﷺ had passed away in which he wrote a letter to the Prophet ﷺ asking why they could not share in their rule; that the Prophet ﷺ should rule one half of the world and he would rule the other half. At that moment, the Prophet ﷺ had a stick in his hand and said, "If he had asked for even this amount of space I would not even give him this much."

When confronted with the army of Musaylamah Kazzāb, which was made up of the tribe of Banū Hanīfah, Sayyidunā Abū Bakr ؓ appointed Sayyidunā Khālid Ibn Al-Walīd ؓ as the general in recognition of the strength of the opposition army. A fierce battle ensued to the extent that ten to eleven thousand of the Sahābah ؓ lost their lives and became *Shahīd* (martyred).

Sayyidunā Khālid Ibn Al-Walīd ؓ extended the invitation of reaccepting Islām to the opposing party on the condition that they would be met with no harm if they chose to do so. This in turn led to many reaffirming their faith and abandoning their posts which led to a severe blow to the opposing army. Those that repented and became sincere Muslims, for them, Allāh ﷻ has promised a goodly reward.

Even when Musaylamah Kazzāb was asked to recite some of the verses revealed to him, after a few days of contemplation he came up with the following :

Elephant, what is an elephant?
Do you know what an elephant is?
It has a long trunk and a small tail?

This was all that he managed to concoct despite his best effort, yet there were those who were so blinded by their loyalty that no amount of evidence would sway them into abandoning their leader.

For others, it was a golden opportunity of redemption and this was the case of Wahshi ﷺ. Before accepting Islām he had martyed one of the best of all of the people, the Prophet's ﷺ beloved uncle, Sayyidunā Hamzah ﷺ. He had been filled with bitter regret when he entered into the fold of Islām and felt that the only way to vindicate himself would be to kill the worst of all people. Allāh ﷻ granted him this honour and he was the one to deal the fatal blow that struck Musaylamah Kazzāb dead. He killed him with his javelin; the same weapon which had been used to martyr the Prophet's ﷺ uncle. This was to bring a little solace to the heart of Sayyidunā Wahshi ؓ as he finally felt that he had made an amendment by killing the worst of all people.

Aswad Anasi was another intruder who made a false claim to be Prophet.

Another group emerged which, just as easily had embraced Islām when it rose to power, were now exited with the death of the Prophet ﷺ and felt that it was no longer a viable source of guidance.

There were those among the ranks of the Muslims who would have joined the expedition in defending the Prophet ﷺ but had remained behind owing to genuine reasons, such as being visually impaired or disabled. For them, Allāh ﷻ absolved them from all blame:

$$\text{لَيْسَ عَلَى الْأَعْمَى حَرَجٌ وَّلَا عَلَى الْأَعْرَجِ حَرَجٌ وَّلَا عَلَى الْمَرِيْضِ حَرَجٌ ۗ وَمَنْ يُّطِعِ اللّٰهَ}$$
$$\text{وَرَسُوْلَهُ يُدْخِلْهُ جَنّٰتٍ تَجْرِيْ مِنْ تَحْتِهَا الْأَنْهَارُ ۚ وَمَنْ يَّتَوَلَّ يُعَذِّبْهُ عَذَابًا اَلِيْمًا}$$

"There is not upon the blind any guilt or upon the lame any guilt or upon the ill any guilt (for remaining behind). And whoever obeys Allāh and His Messenger, He will admit him to gardens beneath which rivers flow, but whoever turns away, He will punish him with a painful punishment." (48:17)

One such example was that of Sayyidunā Abdullāh Ibn Umm Maktūm ؓ who was a blind Companion ؓ. He was keen to join the army but his blindness prevented him from doing so. When the verse, "Not equal are those believers remaining (at home)," was revealed, Sayyidunā Abdullāh Ibn Umme Maktūm ؓ was standing right behind the Prophet ﷺ and asked whether he was exempted from going out to fight to which Allāh ﷻ revealed the following complete verse:

$$ لَا يَسْتَوِي الْقَاعِدُونَ مِنَ الْمُؤْمِنِينَ غَيْرُ أُولِي الضَّرَرِ $$

"Not equal are the believers remaining (at home) other than the disabled." (4:95)

The words revealed were 'Ghairu ulid darar' which absolved those with any form of disability from any blame as they were not able to participate in the battle.

This incident is related in the following Hadīth where Sayyidunā Barā' ؓ said, "When the verse, 'Not equal are the believers who sit (at home)' was revealed, the Messenger of Allāh ﷺ called Zaid and commanded him to write it. Then Ibn Umm Maktūm ؓ came and mentioned he was blind. Allāh ﷻ revealed, 'Ghairu ulid darar' (except those who are disabled (by injury or are blind or lame)." (Bukhāri)

Bukhāri recorded that Sahl Ibn Sa'd ؓ said, "I saw Marwān Ibn al-Hakam sitting in the Masjid. I came and sat by his side. He told us that Zaid Ibn Thābit told him that the Messenger of Allāh ﷺ dictated this verse to him, 'Not equal are the believers who sit (at home) except those who are disabled and those who strive hard and fight in the cause of Allāh 🕮.' Ibn Umm Maktūm 🕮 came to the Prophet 🕮 as he was dictating this very verse to me. Ibn Umm Maktūm 🕮 said, 'O Allāh's Messenger 🕮! By Allāh 🕮, if I had power, I would surely take part in Jihād .' He was a blind man so Allāh 🕮 sent down revelation upon His Messenger 🕮 while his thigh was on mine and it became so heavy for me that I feared that my thigh would be broken. That ended after Allāh 🕮 revealed, 'Ghairu ulid darar' (except those who are disabled)." (Bukhārī)

Those who were left behind in Madīnah Munawwarah owing to some legitimate excuse would still obtain the same reward as those who marched out to fight.

If a person was in the habit of carrying out a good deed and then due to travel or illness was prevented from doing so; they will still be rewarded with the same amount of reward, similar to that of if they had carried out the action whilst they were in good health and able to do so.

Sayyidunā Jābir Ibn Abdullāh Al-Ansārī 🕮 reported: "We accompanied the Prophet 🕮 in an expedition when he said, 'There are some men in Madīnah who are with you wherever you march and whichever valley you cross. They have not joined you in person because of their illness.'" In another version he said, "They share the reward with you." (Muslim)

In another Hadīth, the Prophet 🕮 said, "When a slave falls ill or travels, then he will get a reward similar to that he gets for good deeds practised at home when in good health. (Bukhāri)

A person should always try to carry out as many good deeds as possible in good health and while residing in their own home. When there is a hindrance that deters them from carrying out the action, then the rewards will still be reaped and gained. How Merciful our Lord Allāh ﷻ is, yet many of us still remain heedless and idle; wasting our time away.

When news spread that only those that accompanied the Prophet ﷺ to Hudaybiyah would be able to march with him to Khybar, those with genuine excuses felt that they too would be categorised alongside the hypocrites. Allāh ﷻ clears them and exempts them from participating as they possessed genuine excuses for not going forth. Hence they too deserved the same veneration and respect as those that had marched out to fight against the enemy. Not only this but they would also be entitled to the same reward, for if they were able-bodied, they would never have even contemplated remaining behind.

Obedience to Allāh ﷻ

After describing the category of those that are exempt from fighting, the verse continues:

وَمَن يُطِعِ اللَّهَ وَرَسُولَهُ يُدْخِلْهُ جَنَّتٍ تَجْرِي مِن تَحْتِهَا الْأَنْهَارُ ۖ وَمَن يَتَوَلَّ يُعَذِّبْهُ عَذَابًا أَلِيمًا

"And whoever obeys Allāh and His Messenger, He will admit him into gardens which rivers flow, but whoever turns away, He will punish him with a painful punishment." (48:17)

Obedience to Allāh ﷻ also means obeying His Messenger ﷺ. Both concepts go hand in hand and are united together. Therefore disobedience to the Prophet ﷺ is synonymous to disobeying Allāh ﷻ. Those who submit to the will of Allāh ﷻ and obey Him will enter into Jannah and those that disobey will be made to taste the suffering of chastisement. Allāh ﷻ says:

وَمَن لَّمْ يُؤْمِن بِاللَّهِ وَرَسُولِهِ فَإِنَّا أَعْتَدْنَا لِلْكَافِرِينَ سَعِيرًا

"And whoever has not believed in Allāh and His Messenger, then indeed We have prepared for the disbelievers a blaze." (48:13)

In another verse we find:

إِنَّ الَّذِينَ كَفَرُوا بِآيَاتِنَا سَوْفَ نُصْلِيهِمْ نَارًا كُلَّمَا نَضِجَتْ جُلُودُهُم بَدَّلْنَاهُمْ جُلُودًا غَيْرَهَا لِيَذُوقُوا الْعَذَابَ ۗ إِنَّ اللَّهَ كَانَ عَزِيزًا حَكِيمًا

"Indeed, those who disbelieve in Our verses, We will drive them into a Fire. Every time their skins are roasted through, We will

replace them with other skins so they may taste the punishment. Indeed, Allāh is ever Exalted in Might and Wise." (4:56)

Sayyidunā Abū Hurairah ﷺ narrated that the Messenger of Allāh ﷺ said regarding the fire of Hell, "The fire was ignited for one thousand years until it became red; it was then ignited for one thousand years until it became white; it was then ignited for one thousand years until it became black; it is black and dark." (Tirmidhī, Ibn Mājah)

Paradise

The word Jannāt is plural and is made up of the Arabic letters Jīm and Nūn. Allāh ﷺ has put so much beauty in the Arabic language that any word which has the root letters of Jīm and Nūn has a meaning of concealment. The consonant of the letters are interdependent on each other and knit together to produce an extensive range of words which are in harmony with their definition and meaning. The following are some examples of this:

- Jannah means a garden which is hidden from our eyes.
- Jinn is a creation hidden from our eyes.
- Junūn is an Arabic word for madness which is a hidden illness in a person's mind and cannot be seen.
- Janīn is the Arabic word for the foetus which is hidden in the womb of its mother.
- Junnah is the word for shield which conceals a person from their enemy.

These are but few examples of the richness and depth of the Arabic language.

The verse continues on explaining the beauty of Jannah:

يُدْخِلْهُ جَنَّاتٍ تَجْرِي مِنْ تَحْتِهَا الْأَنْهَارُ

"He will admit him into gardens which rivers flow." (48:17)

The rivers mentioned in Jannah are of four different types:
1. Rivers of Water.
2. Rivers of Milk.
3. Rivers of Honey.
4. Rivers of Wine.

The rivers will remain forever preserved where their taste will never deteriorate or stagnate, remaining pure and unpolluted.
Allāh ﷻ mentions the four different types of rivers while contrasting the strikingly different disparity of the Fire in a bid that we are made to open up our eyes and adhere to His divine commandments:

مَثَلُ الْجَنَّةِ الَّتِي وُعِدَ الْمُتَّقُونَ ۖ فِيهَا أَنْهَارٌ مِّنْ مَّاءٍ غَيْرِ آسِنٍ وَأَنْهَارٌ مِّنْ لَّبَنٍ لَّمْ يَتَغَيَّرْ طَعْمُهُ وَأَنْهَارٌ مِّنْ خَمْرٍ لَّذَّةٍ لِّلشَّارِبِينَ وَأَنْهَارٌ مِّنْ عَسَلٍ مُّصَفًّى ۖ وَلَهُمْ فِيهَا مِنْ كُلِّ الثَّمَرَاتِ وَمَغْفِرَةٌ مِّنْ رَّبِّهِمْ ۖ كَمَنْ هُوَ خَالِدٌ فِي النَّارِ وَسُقُوا مَاءً حَمِيمًا فَقَطَّعَ أَمْعَاءَهُمْ

"Is the description of Paradise which the righteous are promised, wherein are rivers of water unaltered, rivers of milk the taste of which never changes, rivers of wine delicious to those

who drink, and rivers of purified honey, in which they will have from all (kinds of) fruits and forgiveness from their Lord, like (that of) those who abide eternally in the Fire and are given to drink scalding water that will sever their intestines?" (47:15)

And how do we attain Jannah? Two conditions must be met. The first is that we believe in Allāh ﷻ. This consists of following His commands in its entirety and doing righteous actions which will cause us to enter into Jannah. This is described in the following verse:

$$ وَبَشِّرِ الَّذِينَ آمَنُوا وَعَمِلُوا الصَّالِحَاتِ أَنَّ لَهُمْ جَنَّاتٍ تَجْرِي مِنْ تَحْتِهَا الْأَنْهَارُ ۖ كُلَّمَا رُزِقُوا مِنْهَا مِنْ ثَمَرَةٍ رِزْقًا ۙ قَالُوا هَٰذَا الَّذِي رُزِقْنَا مِنْ قَبْلُ ۖ وَأُتُوا بِهِ مُتَشَابِهًا ۖ وَلَهُمْ فِيهَا أَزْوَاجٌ مُطَهَّرَةٌ ۖ وَهُمْ فِيهَا خَالِدُونَ $$

"And give good tidings to those who believe and do righteous deeds that they will have gardens (in Paradise) beneath which rivers flow. Whenever they are provided with a provision of fruit therefrom, they will say, 'this is what we were provided with before.' And it is given to them in likeness. And they will have therein purified spouses and they will abide therein eternally." (2:25)

Heavenly Hospitality

In another verse, Paradise has been described as:

إِنَّ الَّذِيْنَ اٰمَنُوْا وَعَمِلُوا الصَّالِحَاتِ كَانَتْ لَهُمْ جَنَّاتُ الْفِرْدَوْسِ نُزُلًا

"Indeed, those who have believed and done righteous deeds, they will have the Gardens of Paradise as a lodging." (18:107)

The word 'lodging' here is used to describe a place of entertainment and hospitality. When a person thinks of hospitality, they anticipate it to be for a short time and temporary. Also, the question arises that being there for such a vast amount of time may lead to boredom and dullness. Allāh ﷻ puts our mind at ease when He explains:

خَالِدِيْنَ فِيْهَا لَا يَبْغُوْنَ عَنْهَا حِوَلًا

"Wherein they abide eternally. They will not desire from it any transfer." (18:108)

The hospitality in Jannah will be endless. This hospitality and generousity are qualities that are lacking in our societies. Many of us do not even have the care or concern to take the trouble of entertaining and being hospitable to our guests.

Sayyidunā Abū Shurayh Al-'Adawi ؓ said, "I heard with my own two ears and saw with my own two eyes when the Prophet ﷺ spoke and said, 'Whoever believes in Allāh ﷻ and the Last Day, let him honour his guest as he is entitled.' It was said, 'What is his entitlement, O Messenger of Allāh ?' '(The best treatment) for one day and night and hospitality is for three days and anything after that is charity bestowed upon him. And whoever believes in Allāh and the Last Day, let him speak good words or remain silent.'" (Bukhāri)

Once a man came to the Prophet's house. He presented the man with milk from one goat which he drank. He presented milk from a second goat and he finished drinking this also. This continued until the man had drunk the milk of seven goats.

He then took rest for the night. In the morning after he had left, the Prophet realised that the man had soiled the bedding. He started to clean that with his own blessed hands. Not long after the man had left, he realised that he had left his armour behind and returned to the Prophet's house where he found him cleaning the soiled bedding. Being stunned and taken back by what he had just witnessed, he immediately accepted Islām. It was through the exemplary conduct and behaviour of the true Muslims that caused people to accept Islām.

This is a far cry from what we see today. Many of us show little tolerance and are exceedingly averse to any form of inconvenience we may have to endure.

The Beauty of Jannah (Paradise)

When describing what a person will be given in Jannah, the Qur'ān states:

$$لَهُمْ مَّا يَشَآءُوْنَ فِيْهَا وَلَدَيْنَا مَزِيْدٌ$$

"They will have whatever they wish therein, and with Us is more." (50:35)

In another verse it is stated:

$$فَلَا تَعْلَمُ نَفْسٌ مَّا أُخْفِيَ لَهُمْ مِّنْ قُرَّةِ أَعْيُنٍ جَزَآءً بِمَا كَانُوْا يَعْمَلُوْنَ$$

"And no soul knows what has been hidden for them of comfort for eyes as reward for what they used to do. (32:17)

It is related in a Hadīth that the Prophet ﷺ said, "Paradise has one hundred grades, each of which is big as the distance between heaven and earth. The highest of them is Firdaws, and the best of them is Firdaws. The throne is above Firdaws and from it springs forth the rivers of Paradise. If you ask Allāh ﷻ, ask him for Firdaws." (Ibn Mājah)

In a Hadīth Qudsī, it is reported regarding the beauty of Jannah. Sayyidunā Abū Hurairah ؆ reported that the Messenger of Allāh ﷺ said, "Allāh ﷻ the Most High said: 'I have prepared for My righteous servants what no eye has seen, no ear has heard, and no heart can ever imagine.' The Prophet ﷺ then said, 'If you wish, recite, no person knows what is kept hidden for them of joy as a reward for what they used to do." (32:10) (Bukhāri, Muslim)

In Jannah, a person will get everything they desired and wished for. Their minds will be infinite and unlimited; there will be no boundaries or parameters. Also, from these Ahādīth we learn that when asking Allāh ﷻ for Jannah, we should ask for Jannatul Firdaws which is the highest level of Paradise.

In the Qur'ān, when Allāh ﷻ mentions a proposition, it is accompanied by a counter proposition which denotes a direct contrast to the original proposition. The use of the literary device of antithesis is common in verses mentioning the Hereafter. Where Jannah's delights are mentioned, it is immediately contrasted with Jahannam's torment and vice versa.

Hope and Fear

نَبِّئْ عِبَادِيٓ أَنِّيٓ أَنَا ٱلْغَفُورُ ٱلرَّحِيمُ ﴿٤٩﴾ وَأَنَّ عَذَابِي هُوَ ٱلْعَذَابُ ٱلْأَلِيمُ ﴿٥٠﴾

"(O Muhammad), inform My servants that it is I Who am the Forgiving, the Merciful. And that it is My punishment which is a painful punishment." (15:49-50)

In the above verse we can see the contrast between Allāh ﷻ Punishment and the mentioning of His Mercy.

Īmān (faith) resides between both hope and fear. The intelligent person is the one who subdues his Nafs and prepares themselves for the Hereafter. The foolish person is the one who follows his Nafs, and when prompted to fulfil his obligations takes no heed saying, "Allāh ﷻ is Forgiving and Merciful."

The person fails to contemplate the concept of the type of people Allāh ﷻ will forgive. He has made it clear that He will shower His mercy on those who put in effort, yet despite their best effort they falter and make mistakes.

Allāh ﷻ will turn to these people in compassion and forgiveness, unlike the person who remains complacent, conceited and self-satisfied without even making an attempt to implement that which Allāh ﷻ has commanded and ordered, being neglectful of all his duties and responsibilities and then expecting Allāh ﷻ to show compassion and leniency towards him.

Our pious predecessors lived their lives fearing Allāh ﷻ but at their time of departure from this world, they had more hope in the Mercy of Allāh ﷻ as opposed to fear.

When death approached Imām Ahmad Ibn Hanbal ؓ, he called his son Abdullāh and said, "Read those Ahādīth which mention Allāh's ﷻ Mercy, Compassion and Kindness. I want to listen to them and meet Allāh ﷻ having good opinion and thoughts regarding Him.

A person who has more fear of Allāh ﷻ will be able to better safe-guard themselves from falling into the pitfall of sin. This will lead them to strive and struggle in the path of Allāh so that when the time to take leave from this world arrives, they will call out to Allāh ﷻ in the hope that He will show greater compassion and leniency. This is why we should live upon fear and die upon hope.

Three Types of 'Aql (Intellect)

People possess varying degrees of intellectual abilities and capacities and Allāh ﷻ will not take a person to task for what is beyond a person's means and level of ability and comprehension. There are three types of 'Aql (intellect):

1. **Kāmilul Aql:** This is when a person has a sound mind and the ability to understand, perceive and comprehend things around them.
2. **Nāqisul Aql:** A person has intellect but has a reduced level of ability to interpret and grasp things.
3. **Fāqidul Aql:** This is a condition when a person has a deformity which causes a defect in their intellect; hence their reasoning abilities are severely impaired and diminished. These are the people who will be granted Jannah without any reckoning.

Each person will be dealt by Allāh ﷻ in accordance to their level of reasoning and understanding.

Remaining Steadfast

After addressing those who believe, Allāh ﷻ says to believe in what
He has sent down:

$$\text{يَٰٓأَيُّهَا الَّذِينَ ءَامَنُوٓا۟ ءَامِنُوا۟ بِٱللَّهِ وَرَسُولِهِ وَٱلۡكِتَٰبِ ٱلَّذِي نَزَّلَ عَلَىٰ رَسُولِهِ وَٱلۡكِتَٰبِ ٱلَّذِيٓ أَنزَلَ مِن قَبۡلُ ۚ وَمَن يَكۡفُرۡ بِٱللَّهِ وَمَلَٰٓئِكَتِهِ وَكُتُبِهِ وَرُسُلِهِ وَٱلۡيَوۡمِ ٱلۡأٓخِرِ فَقَدۡ ضَلَّ ضَلَٰلَۢا بَعِيدًا}$$

**"O you who have believed, believe in Allāh and His Messenger
and the Book that He sent down upon His Messenger and the
Scripture which He sent down before. And whoever disbelieves
in Allāh, His angels, His books, His Messengers and the Last
Day has certainly gone far astray." (4:136)**

A believer after embracing Islām needs to remain steadfast on Īmān
until death. In order for us to reach this level, we must strive to instil
these characteristics within ourselves.

When we recited the Kalimah, *'Lā ilāha illal lāhu Muhammadur
Rasūlullāh'* (There is no god but Allāh ﷻ and Muhammad ﷺ is the
Messenger of Allāh ﷺ), this came with conditions in the form of a
complete package. We must obey Allāh ﷻ and follow the Sunnah of
our beloved Prophet ﷺ. We don't have the discretion to pick and
choose what we wish to follow.

Similar to the example of a man who at the time of his marriage contract accepts and agrees to the marriage. Now he is obliged to provide the maintenance and expenditure for his wife. If his wife becomes ill, he has the duty to take care of her needs. He cannot neglect or forsake her in an attempt to discard and cast aside his responsibilities. A marriage contract is an agreement and a commitment and the associated responsibilities must be discharged.

In the Battle of Badr the believers were small in number; a small band of 313 men ill-equipped and outnumbered, fighting a greater force of 1000 men who were well equipped and possessed a greater number of weapons and cavalry. Not knowing what fate awaited them, they put their trust in Allāh ﷻ and were met with victory.

The next battle they fought was the Battle of Uhud, and although they suffered a setback and suffered heavy casualties as a result of misunderstanding the Prophet's ﷺ orders, lessons were learnt and they came back with greater resilience and fervour in wanting to please the Prophet ﷺ in redressing the blunder.

At the time of the peace treaty, their forces were strengthened and greater in number and they felt that they stood unrivalled in comparison to the disbelievers. They felt that they could defeat them in one swift stroke. This is what aggravated and intensified the situation for the Sahābah ؓ in that they found it difficult to understand why the Prophet ﷺ agreed to terms and conditions that they felt were humiliating when they thought that the enemy could easily be defeated and subdued.

When they were small in number at the time of the Battle of Badr and their future was uncertain, they stood their ground and remained firm. Now, when they had nothing to lose, they had to agree to what they felt were humiliating conditions in agreeing to the terms of the treaty.

What were they to do when they were all made to feel that there was a great grievance being committed? How could they just stand by and allow the disbelievers to feel they have the upper hand. This even led to Sayyidunā Umar ؓ asking the Prophet ﷺ the following questions: "Are we not on the truth and our enemies on falsehood?" The Prophet ﷺ replied, "Yes." "Are you not the true Prophet?" The Prophet ﷺ replied in response, " Yes, do you have any doubt about it?" Sayyidunā Umar ؓ answered, "No, but why should we be disgraced in this way? Did you not say we are going to go for Umrah?" The Prophet ﷺ said, "Yes, but did I say this year?" Sayyidunā Umar ؓ could not contain himself. He was very passionate when it came to defending the truth and could not understand the underlying wisdom as to why the Prophet ﷺ had accepted the conditions of the treaty. However, regardless of his inner feelings, he stood by the Prophet ﷺ.

Despite their inability to understand the situation at hand, they upheld and defended whatever course of action the Prophet ﷺ took when he signed the Treaty of Hudaybiyah. Little did they realise that by adhering to obey the Prophet ﷺ even at the time they felt there could have been a more preferable course of action, won the pleasure of Allāh ﷻ to such an extent that not only did He inform them that He was pleased with them but the Treaty of Hudaybiyah was a triumph and soon they would achieve victory upon victory and be recompensed with the booty and spoils of war.

Imagine the pleasure and sheer delight the Sahābah ؓ would have felt upon hearing this news of glad tidings and imminent success. Because of their patience and perseverance, Allāh ﷻ was announcing the success they would accomplish in the near future. This undoubtedly would have been a boost to their morale and made them even more eager and determined in displaying their sense of obligation and gratitude.

The Spread of Islām

The Treaty of Hudaybiyah paved the way to two years where peace prevailed. Hence Islām spread rapidly around the surrounding territories and grew from strength to strength. The number of believers also grew rapidly making Islām dominant. The political climate of the history of Islām was changed forever, gaining firm recognition throughout the world.

This was the first time many were able to get a closer analysis and gain a more profound and accurate understanding of what Islām truly represented. People were able to observe the temperament and the disposition of the Muslims in full swing. This led to masses of people flocking towards Islām. In these two consecutive years, more people accepted this faith in comparison to the 19 years before the Prophet ﷺ calling people to Islām.

Many times an event may take place but we are unable to see the underlying wisdom behind this. We need to ultimately put our trust in Allāh ﷻ and know that everything that is to befall us, whether good or evil, will surely come to pass and anything that was not intended for us, will never occur. We are further reminded of this in the following verses:

وَمَغَانِمَ كَثِيرَةً يَأْخُذُونَهَا ۗ وَكَانَ اللَّهُ عَزِيزًا حَكِيمًا ﴿١٩﴾ وَعَدَكُمُ اللَّهُ مَغَانِمَ كَثِيرَةً تَأْخُذُونَهَا فَعَجَّلَ لَكُمْ هَٰذِهِ وَكَفَّ أَيْدِيَ النَّاسِ عَنكُمْ وَلِتَكُونَ آيَةً لِّلْمُؤْمِنِينَ وَيَهْدِيَكُمْ صِرَاطًا مُّسْتَقِيمًا ﴿٢٠﴾ وَأُخْرَىٰ لَمْ تَقْدِرُوا عَلَيْهَا قَدْ أَحَاطَ اللَّهُ بِهَا ۚ وَكَانَ اللَّهُ عَلَىٰ كُلِّ شَيْءٍ قَدِيرًا ﴿٢١﴾

"And much war booty which they will take. And ever is Allah Exalted in Might and Wise. Allāh has promised you much booty that you will take (in the future) and has hastened for you this (victory) and withheld the hands of people from you, that it may be a sign for the believers and (that) He may guide you to a straight path. And (He promises) other (victories) that you were (so far) unable to (realise) which Allāh has already encompassed. And ever is Allāh over all things, Competent." (48:19-21)

Sayyidunā Abdullāh Ibn Abbās ؓ said that this does not only refer to the expedition of Khaybar but could refer to any battle right up until the Day of Judgement.

Many opportunities will present themselves and much booty will be acquired for those who strive in the path of Allāh ﷻ to make His Dīn supreme and safeguard it from corruption.

The first way Islām became dominant was at the time of the Prophet ﷺ through the proof and authenticity of Islām being a divine religion. This continued through the leadership of Sayyidunā Umar ﵁. Sayyidunā Umar ﵁ ruled for 10 years, in which vast regions of the world came under his control in just a short period. The Sahābah ﵃ could not imagine that they would defeat the superpowers of the Roman and Persian empires. Muslims continued to rule for over 1300 years until the Caliphate was destroyed on Monday 3rd March 1924 (28th Rajab 1342 AD).

The third stage of dominance will take place when Muslims will rise to power when Imam Mahdi will arrive on this earth. Allāh ﷻ only possesses the knowledge of when this event shall come to pass.

Weakness of Faith

Allāh ﷻ states the condition of the disbelievers that their weakness would have resulted in them absconding and fleeing from the battleground.

وَلَوْ قَٰتَلَكُمُ الَّذِينَ كَفَرُوا لَوَلَّوُا الْأَدْبَٰرَ ثُمَّ لَا يَجِدُونَ وَلِيًّا وَّلَا نَصِيْرًا

"And if those (Makkans) who disbelieve had fought with you,
they would have turned their backs. Then they would not find
any protector or a helper." (48:22)

Allāh's ﷻ greater underlying wisdom prevented the believers from
engaging in battle with the disbelievers. The disbelievers prevented
the Muslims from moving forward. Allāh ﷻ consoles and supports
the believers, reassuring them that relief and ease will follow and
there would be other victories to follow.

It was not the number of believers that was important, but instead
the sincerity and conviction of their faith and that was in their
hearts. This was the determining factor for success. Allāh ﷻ explains
this in another verse:

كَمْ مِّنْ فِئَةٍ قَلِيْلَةٍ غَلَبَتْ فِئَةً كَثِيْرَةً بِإِذْنِ اللهِ ۚ وَاللهُ مَعَ الصّٰبِرِيْنَ

"And how many a small group has overcome a large group by
permission of Allāh. And Allāh is with the patient." (2:249)

This verse refers to the small army of Sayyidunā Dāwūd عليه السلام who
were able to overpower the mighty enemy of Jālūt and his followers;
placing their complete trust in Allāh ﷻ and standing firm in the face
of trials and tribulations.

Condition of the Disbelievers

Allāh ﷻ describes the condition of the hearts of the disbelievers:

لَا يُقَٰتِلُونَكُمْ جَمِيعًا إِلَّا فِي قُرًى مُّحَصَّنَةٍ أَوْ مِن وَرَآءِ جُدُرٍ بَأْسُهُم بَيْنَهُمْ شَدِيدٌ تَحْسَبُهُمْ جَمِيعًا وَقُلُوبُهُمْ شَتَّىٰ ذَٰلِكَ بِأَنَّهُمْ قَوْمٌ لَّا يَعْقِلُونَ

"They will not fight you all except within fortified cities or from behind walls. Their violence among themselves is severe. You think they are together but their hearts are diverse. That is because they are people who do not reason." (59:14)

Allāh ﷻ tells us the condition of the disbelievers that were fighting against the Prophet ﷺ. The meaning can also be understood in general sense that there is disunity and division amongst them. Externally they appear unified and united, but in their hearts, their own agendas and policies take precedence and are given priority when it comes to the critical point of disclosure. We see the wisdom behind this unravel when we are made to reflect on the extraordinary and expansive spread of Islām within the short space of two years.

Paving the way to Victory

Allāh ﷻ says:

بَلْ نَقْذِفُ بِالْحَقِّ عَلَى الْبَٰطِلِ فَيَدْمَغُهُ فَإِذَا هُوَ زَاهِقٌ

"We dash the truth upon falsehood and it destroys it and there-

upon it departs." (21:18)

In another verse Allāh ﷻ says:

وَقُلْ جَآءَ الْحَقُّ وَزَهَقَ الْبَاطِلُ إِنَّ الْبَاطِلَ كَانَ زَهُوقًا

"And say, 'Truth has come and falsehood has departed.' Indeed is falsehood (by nature) ever bound to depart." (17:81)

Further to this Allāh ﷻ says:

اِسْتِكْبَارًا فِي الْأَرْضِ وَمَكْرَ السَّيِّئِ وَلَا يَحِيقُ الْمَكْرُ السَّيِّئُ إِلَّا بِأَهْلِهِ فَهَلْ يَنْظُرُونَ إِلَّا سُنَّتَ الْأَوَّلِينَ فَلَنْ تَجِدَ لِسُنَّتِ اللهِ تَبْدِيلًا وَلَنْ تَجِدَ لِسُنَّتِ اللهِ تَحْوِيلًا

"But you will never find in the way of Allāh any change and you will never find in the way of Allāh any alteration." (35:43)

Power continuously revolves and rotates in the hands of the believers as well as the disbelievers. The believers however, will ultimately be victorious. Allāh ﷻ reminds us that we too will taste success and triumph if we follow Allāh ﷻ and His Messenger ﷺ.

Even though at times the truth seems to be subdued, in the end, it will triumph and overpower any falsehood. The truth always becomes victorious and will reign supreme. Allāh ﷻ says:

قُلِ اللّٰهُمَّ مَالِكَ الْمُلْكِ تُؤْتِي الْمُلْكَ مَنْ تَشَآءُ وَتَنْزِعُ الْمُلْكَ مِمَّنْ تَشَآءُ وَتُعِزُّ مَنْ تَشَآءُ

وَتُذِلُّ مَنْ تَشَاءُ بِيَدِكَ الْخَيْرُ إِنَّكَ عَلَى كُلِّ شَيْءٍ قَدِيرٌ

"Say 'Allāh, Owner of sovereignty. You give sovereignty to whom You will and You take sovereignty away from whom You will. You honour whom You will and humble whom You will. In Your Hand is all good. Indeed, You are over all things Competent.'" (3:26)

Those who have full conviction and belief (the true friends of Allāh ﷻ and the pious) are those whom Allāh ﷻ will grant victory.

هُوَ الَّذِيَ أَرْسَلَ رَسُوْلَهُ بِالْهُدَى وَدِيْنِ الْحَقِّ لِيُظْهِرَهُ عَلَى الدِّيْنِ كُلِّهِ وَلَوْ كَرِهَ الْمُشْرِكُوْنَ

"It is He Who has sent His Messenger with guidance and the religion of truth to manifest it all over religions, although those who associate others with Allāh dislike it." (9:33)

Prior to the commencement of the Day of Judgement, Imām Mahdi and Sayyidunā Īsā ﷺ will come and the truth will once again become established and reign supreme.

Allāh ﷻ did not want a battle to break out in the place of Hudaybiyah. This is further elucidated in the following verses:

سُنَّةَ اللهِ الَّتِيْ قَدْ خَلَتْ مِنْ قَبْلُ وَلَنْ تَجِدَ لِسُنَّةِ اللهِ تَبْدِيْلًا ﴿٢٣﴾ وَهُوَ الَّذِيْ كَفَّ أَيْدِيَهُمْ عَنْكُمْ وَأَيْدِيَكُمْ عَنْهُم بِبَطْنِ مَكَّةَ مِنْ بَعْدِ أَنْ أَظْفَرَكُمْ عَلَيْهِمْ وَكَانَ اللهُ بِمَا تَعْمَلُوْنَ بَصِيْرًا ﴿٢٤﴾ هُمُ الَّذِيْنَ كَفَرُوْا وَصَدُّوْكُمْ عَنِ الْمَسْجِدِ الْحَرَامِ وَالْهَدْيَ مَعْكُوْفًا

106

أَن يَبْلُغَ مَحِلَّهُ ۚ وَلَوْلَا رِجَالٌ مُّؤْمِنُونَ وَنِسَاءٌ مُّؤْمِنَاتٌ لَّمْ تَعْلَمُوهُمْ أَن تَطَئُوهُمْ فَتُصِيبَكُم
مِّنْهُم مَّعَرَّةٌ بِغَيْرِ عِلْمٍ ۚ لِيُدْخِلَ اللَّهُ فِي رَحْمَتِهِ مَن يَشَاءُ ۚ لَوْ تَزَيَّلُوا لَعَذَّبْنَا الَّذِينَ كَفَرُوا
مِنْهُمْ عَذَابًا أَلِيمًا ﴿٢٥﴾

"(This is) the established way of Allāh which has occurred before. And never will you find in the way of Allāh any change. And it is He Who withheld their hands from you and your hands from them in (the area of) Makkah after He caused you to overcome them. Allāh is always Watchful over what you do. They are the ones who disbelieved and obstructed you from Masjid Haram while the sacrificial animals were restrained from reaching its place of sacrifice. And if not for believing men and believing women whom you did not know that you might trample them, and you unknowingly suffer harm on their account, the matter would have been concluded (you would have been permitted to enter Makkah). (This was so) That Allāh might admit to His Mercy whom He willed. If they had been apart (from them), We would have punished those who disbelieved among them with a painful punishment." (48:23-25)**

Sayyidunā Salamah Ibn Al-Akwa ﷺ says, "I was lying down under a tree. Four polytheists had gathered together and were plotting against the Prophet ﷺ. I got so angry, but then I thought to myself that we have made the peace treaty, so how could I get revenge?" He took the words of the Prophet ﷺ into consideration, remembering the declaration of the peace treaty and decided not to act.

As he sat under another tree, the thought lingered on in his mind. When the polytheists had fallen asleep, he drew out his sword. He brought the perpetrators forth to the Prophet ﷺ and explained how these people had been swearing; insulting and abusing the Prophet ﷺ. The Prophet ﷺ turned to Sayyidunā Salamah Ibn Al-Akwa ؓ and said, "Let them go."

At that moment, Sayyidunā Salamah Ibn Al-Akwa's ؓ uncle Sayyidunā Āmir ؓ had got hold of 70 of the polytheists who were plotting against the Prophet ﷺ. The Sahābah ؓ asked the Prophet ﷺ what action they should take and the Prophet ﷺ said, "Forgive them." At the same time, from the mountain of Tan'īm, 80 disbelievers had gathered and they too were conspiring against the Prophet ﷺ. Again, these people were captured and brought forth to the Prophet ﷺ but the very same command to forgive and set them free was given.

The Prophet ﷺ had now entered into a peace treaty with the idolaters of Makkah Mukarramah and would uphold and honour it, resisting any provocation.

The verse mentions a reason why Allāh ﷻ kept the believers from fighting the disbelievers. This was because amongst the disbelievers there were those who had secretly converted to Islām and had concealed their faith. There was the danger that they too would have been subject to attack and harmed. This would have been detrimental to the believers even though the believers were not aware of the concealed faith of the new converts. To avoid any harm from befalling the believers who had concealed their faith, Allāh ﷻ commanded the Prophet ﷺ to withdraw and put into place these measures, which ultimately paved the way to victory for the Muslims.

Scholars mention that the number of people who had concealed their faith amounted to nine people made up of seven men and two women. How incredible was the status of these nine people that Allāh ﷻ prevented an entire battle from taking place to protect them!

Rules of Warfare

In our current situation of warfare, we see that innocent civilians including children are not spared. Bombs are dropped indiscriminately killing and destroying lands and everything contained within. Large areas, buildings including schools and hospitals are not even spared. How low humanity has sunk that when it comes to warfare, evil and wrongdoing not only becomes authorised but acceptable.

There are limits set by Allāh ﷻ in regards to a battle. Those directly involved in the battle may be fought but women or children must not be killed or harmed. People in places of worship, the elderly and those who have no involvement in the battle must be protected. Even the animals must also remain unhurt and free from injury and maltreatment. Trees and plantation cannot be uprooted and cut down. These are some of the beautiful teachings of Islām.

Innocence and Protection

From the Aqīdah of the Ahlus-Sunnah wal-Jamā'at is that we believe all the Prophets were Ma'sūm (sinless) and the Sahābah ﷺ were Mahfūz (safeguarded) in the subjective sense of divine decree. Allāh ﷻ preserved and protected them from committing immoral acts of wrongdoing, transgression and from falling into deviancy. If they made a mistake, they sought immediate amendment and rectification so that any error or oversight could not manifest itself and take hold.

By not allowing the Sahābah ﷺ to fight as a result of not being allowed entry into the Masjid Haram, safeguarded them from committing great harm. This would have included the nine secret believers.

The Arabic word used in verse is ma'arrah, which can have the following three meanings:
1. **Sin**: If they had fought, the believers might have mistakenly killed the other believers who had concealed their faith.
2. **Harm**: A battle would have led to damage and injury.
3. **Difficulty**: This could have caused great distress and anguish upon the realisation that the believers had actually harmed and

killed the people who had concealed their faith. This in turn would have led to prolonged trauma and suffering.

In the verse where Allāh ﷻ mentions that he wanted to admit them into His mercy, this is not only referring to the nine believers who had concealed their faith but also those that would also eventually embrace Islām after being enlightened by its true teachings.

The Prophet ﷺ also encountered a similar situation in Tā'if which he described as the hardest point of his life. This was worse than the day of Uhud where he had been drained of all his mental and physical strength and suffering at the time from the effects of the recent deaths of his beloved wife Sayyidah Khadījah ﷺ and his uncle Abū Tālib. Here he had sought protection, but not only had the leaders reviled and rebuked his message, they also had the youth of the town chase him out, pelting him with stones to the extent that his blessed feet were covered in blood. At this point, Allāh ﷻ ordered an angel to be sent and if the Prophet ﷺ commanded, the whole of the city of Tā'if would have been destroyed. The Prophet ﷺ still refused to see them harmed saying that even if they did not accept the message, then he hoped that their progeny would embrace the message and teachings.

The trials and tribulations they faced and underwent would provide humanity with an example on how we too must undergo the hardships of life's struggles if we are to be rewarded with eternal success.

The verse continues saying that if however, these nine people were separate from the polytheists, then nothing could have stopped Allāh's ﷻ punishment from descending. As a result of these blessed people, the entire community was saved and later people went on to embrace Islām in their thousands. Within a short space of two years, the Prophet ﷺ marched forward with 10,000 men and conquered Makkah Mukarramah.

Even if we look at the social ills manifest in today's society, we cannot help but think that it is perhaps the Du'ās of the few God-fearing people amongst us that has averted Allāh's ﷻ wrath and punishment from descending upon us.

Arrogance and Ignorance

The disbelievers prevented the Muslims entry to the Masjid Haram due to the pride and arrogance they harboured in their hearts. The verse continues explaining the matter further:

إِذْ جَعَلَ الَّذِيْنَ كَفَرُوْا فِيْ قُلُوْبِهِمُ الْحَمِيَّةَ حَمِيَّةَ الْجَٰهِلِيَّةِ فَأَنْزَلَ اللهُ سَكِيْنَتَهُ عَلَىٰ رَسُوْلِهِ وَعَلَى الْمُؤْمِنِيْنَ وَأَلْزَمَهُمْ كَلِمَةَ التَّقْوَىٰ وَكَانُوْا أَحَقَّ بِهَا وَأَهْلَهَا وَكَانَ اللهُ بِكُلِّ شَيْءٍ عَلِيْمًا

"When those who disbelieved had put into their hearts disdain – the disdain of the time of ignorance. But Allāh sent down His tranquillity upon His Messenger and upon the believers and imposed upon them the Word of righteousness and they were more deserving of it and worthy of it. And ever is Allāh of all

things Knowing ." (48:26)

Their aggressive patriotic sentiments and their pride of nationalism prevented them from allowing the believers to enter the Masjid Harām. Their own tribal affiliations prevented them from acknowledging the truth which stemmed from deep-rooted arrogance.

The Arabic word used is *'Hamiyyatul Jāhiliyyah'* to describe the disdain they had in their hearts in the time of ignorance. Hamiyyah itself is acceptable in the form of showing patriotism and nationalism to one's country if it does not involve arrogance and ignorance. In this verse, Hamiyyatul Jāhiliyyah refers to that passion of patriotism and nationalism where there is no restriction. Patriotic feelings and sentiments should not stand in the way of addressing a wrong when it is committed.

A person's love for their country of origin may lead to them committing acts of transgression. For example, a person acts unjustly to faithfully support a person on the account that they are from the same village instead of addressing the problem. This is a form of Hamiyyatul Jāhiliyyah which is forbidden in Islām.

Jahl is the opposite of possessing *'Aql* (intellect), i.e. not having the knowledge. It also possesses the meaning of not restricting oneself; being unmindful and without consideration of the consequences. Heedlessness in Dīn procures the greatest threat to a person's well being not only in this life; but also in the next.

The following example clarifies this point further:

وَإِذْ قَالَ مُوسَىٰ لِقَوْمِهِ إِنَّ اللَّهَ يَأْمُرُكُمْ أَن تَذْبَحُوا بَقَرَةً ۖ قَالُوا أَتَتَّخِذُنَا هُزُوًا ۖ قَالَ أَعُوذُ بِاللَّهِ أَنْ أَكُونَ مِنَ الْجَهِلِينَ

"And recall when Mūsā said to his people, 'Indeed, Allāh commands you to slaughter a cow.' They said, 'Do you take us in ridicule?' He said, 'I seek refuge in Allāh from being among the ignorant.'" (2:67)

This verse was revealed when a dispute had arisen over the death of a man who was murdered. The people turned to their Prophet, Sayyidunā Mūsā ﷺ to resolve the issue. This was when the above verse was revealed. The people were not able to comprehend the significance of slaughtering a cow which would lead to the discovery of the murderer's identity. Instead, they began questioning Sayyidunā Mūsā ﷺ in disbelief. This in turn led Sayyidunā Mūsā ﷺ showing substantial annoyance and anger to the extent that he sought refuge in Allāh ﷻ from falling into *Jāhiliyyah* (ignorance).

Sayyidunā Mūsā ﷺ was endowed with great knowledge and wisdom. The ignorance which is being referred to here is not ignorance regarding knowledge but from the ignorance of impulsive behaviour. Unrestrained intelligence is when a person does what he feels is right, regardless of whether it is allowed or prohibited. In today's society, we are at liberty to do as we please but we are distant from the consequences of our actions that we will have to answer for.

Types of Ignorance

Jāhilliyah means ignorance in the form of unrestrained thoughts. This is divided into four types which are as follows:

Hamiyyatul Jāhiliyyah: The passion of patriotism and nationalism as previously discussed.

Zannul Jāhiliyyah: Possessing Zann (thoughts) which are good are acceptable but to carry thoughts of Zannul Jāhiliyyah is sinful. An example of this is during the time of the Battle of Uhud. The Muslims had suffered heavy losses to the point that some began to question whether or not they had made the right choice in coming out in support of the Prophet ﷺ.

The Munāfiqūn were quick in spreading their thoughts that if the believers not gone out in following the Prophet ﷺ, they would not have got killed. Now some were questioning their actions on account of the loss they had suffered of whether or not it was the right decision. Allāh ﷻ responded by saying that those for whom death was decreed would have encountered their fate even if they were in their houses. This is reflected in the following verse:

وَلَن يُؤَخِّرَ اللَّهُ نَفْسًا إِذَا جَآءَ أَجَلُهَا ۚ وَاللَّهُ خَبِيرٌ بِمَا تَعْمَلُونَ

"But never will Allāh delay a soul when its time has come. And Allāh is acquainted with what you do." (63:11)

115

Even for those who thought they were safe by concealing themselves, Allāh ﷻ says:

أَيْنَ مَا تَكُونُوا يُدْرِككُّمُ الْمَوْتُ وَلَوْ كُنتُمْ فِى بُرُوجٍ مُّشَيَّدَةٍ وَإِن تُصِبْهُمْ حَسَنَةٌ يَقُولُوا
هَٰذِهِ مِنْ عِندِ اللَّهِ وَإِن تُصِبْهُمْ سَيِّئَةٌ يَقُولُوا هَٰذِهِ مِنْ عِندِكَ قُلْ كُلٌّ مِّنْ عِندِ اللَّهِ فَمَالِ
هَٰؤُلَاءِ الْقَوْمِ لَا يَكَادُونَ يَفْقَهُونَ حَدِيثًا

"Wherever you may be, death will overtake you even if you should be within towers of lofty construction. But if good comes to them, they say, 'This is from Allāh' and if evil befalls them they say, 'This is from you.' Say, 'All (things) are from Allāh.' So what is (the matter) with those people that they can hardly understand any statement?" (4:78)

The thoughts they possessed was that of Zannul Jāhiliyyah. Similar to a person who studies the Dīn and becomes a qualified scholar but then feels someone has achieved much greater success in worldly matters by having achieved a qualification in another academic field. By comparing themselves in this manner, they are belittling the Dīn of Allāh ﷻ.

Tabarrujjul Jāhiliyyah: Dressing to display oneself. This includes dressing immodestly in tight-fitting clothing or exposing those parts of the body that Allāh ﷻ has ordered to be covered and concealed. This is to avoid attracting and drawing attention to oneself and so to dress in a way that is contrary to Allāh's ﷻ orders falls in the category of Tabarrujjul Jāhiliyyah.

Beautifying oneself is an inherent natural quality, particularly within women and there is no issue if it is done in front of those whom it is permissible to freely mix with.

Hukmul Jāhiliyyah: When referring to the Hukm (order), a person uses wisdom to derive a ruling from an order. This action is commendable but if the action is unrestrained and a ruling is sought according to one's own desires, then this is when it falls into the forbidden category of Hukmul Jāhiliyyah.

For example, a person feels attracted to the same sex. They now feel they have the right to act upon that feeling purely based on their lusts and inclinations. This concept of being at liberty to choose without there being any consequences is actually taking the fact of Allāh's ﷻ divine law out of the equation.

Our preoccupation with exploring the universe has made the concept of the existence of God take a back seat in our minds. The desire for the accumulation of wealth and riches of the world with its glitter and glamour has overtaken our concern for the Hereafter. Our bodies have become the subject of exemplary beatification to the extent that vast amounts of our energy and wealth are used in polishing our outward appearances, yet our inward souls are neglected and left to decay and perish. One person's thoughts can have an effect on the actions of an entire system at work. Where 'Aql (intellect) is unable to push forward, this is where Wahī (divine revelation) takes charge in guiding us. Human intellect is limited therefore revelation becomes sovereign as it is unfailing in guiding us to the straight path.

The Word of Righteousness (Kalimatut Taqwā)

After explaining the disdain of the time of ignorance the disbelievers had in their hearts, the verse continues explaining the contrasting characteristics felt by the believers:

إِذْ جَعَلَ الَّذِينَ كَفَرُوا فِي قُلُوبِهِمُ الْحَمِيَّةَ حَمِيَّةَ الْجَاهِلِيَّةِ فَأَنزَلَ اللهُ سَكِينَتَهُ عَلَى رَسُولِهِ وَعَلَى الْمُؤْمِنِينَ وَأَلْزَمَهُمْ كَلِمَةَ التَّقْوَى وَكَانُوا أَحَقَّ بِهَا وَأَهْلَهَا وَكَانَ اللهُ بِكُلِّ شَيْءٍ عَلِيمًا

"But Allāh sent down His tranquillity upon His Messenger and upon the believers and imposed upon them the word of righteousness and they were more deserving of it and worthy of it. And ever is Allāh of all things knowing." (48:26)

Serenity and peace descended upon the Prophet ﷺ and the believers from Allāh ﷻ. The Arabic word used to describe the word of righteousness is *Kalimatut taqwā*. Sūfīs (spiritual mentors) describe the five levels and stages of Taqwā:

1. The station (Maqām) of Islām - a person guards against disbelief.
2. The station of repentance (Tawbah) - one guards themselves against sins and forbidden acts.
3. The station of scrupulousness (Warā) - one guards against doubtful matters.
4. The station of worldly detachment (Zuhd) - guarding oneself

against what is lawful i.e. unnecessary to one's needs.

5. The station of spiritually witnessing Allāh 🕮 (Mushāhadah) - one guards the heart against other than Allāh 🕮 being present (Hudhūr ghairullāh) in it.

What Allāh 🕮 Wills

The Prophet 🕮 had dreamt that he would enter Makkah Mukarramah and perform Umrah but Allāh 🕮 did not show the exact time of this event. As previously mentioned, the Prophet's 🕮 dreams were true visions which foretold the events that would come to pass. Allāh 🕮 says:

$$\text{لَقَدْ صَدَقَ اللّٰهُ رَسُوْلَهُ الرُّءْيَا بِالْحَقِّ لَتَدْخُلُنَّ الْمَسْجِدَ الْحَرَامَ إِنْ شَآءَ اللّٰهُ اٰمِنِيْنَ}$$

$$\text{مُحَلِّقِيْنَ رُءُوْسَكُمْ وَمُقَصِّرِيْنَ لَا تَخَافُوْنَ ۖ فَعَلِمَ مَالَمْ تَعْلَمُوْا فَجَعَلَ مِنْ دُوْنِ ذٰلِكَ فَتْحًا}$$

$$\text{قَرِيْبًا}$$

"Certainly has Allāh showed to His Messenger the vision in truth. You will surely enter Masjid Harām if Allāh wills in safety, with your heads shaved and (hair) shortened, not fearing (anyone). He knew what you did not know and has arranged before that a conquest near (at hand)." (48:27)

Allāh 🕮 uses the past perfect tense to demonstrate that something is surely going to happen. The phrase that tells the Muslims they will without a doubt enter has been revealed in the future tense in a manner which refers to something destined in the near future.

After mentioning that the believers would perform Umrah, the verse continues with 'Inshā-Allāh' (if Allāh ﷺ wills). At first sight, a person may be struck as to why these words have been revealed in this manner, but this is to further remind the believer that nothing can take place without the will of Allāh ﷺ.

Allāh ﷺ has power over all things and He is imparting the knowledge that nothing should be carried out without us first mentioning the words Inshā-Allāh. This is first and foremost a reminder to ourselves that every plan is according to Allāh's ﷺ will and without His leave, no power can frustrate it.

By saying the words Inshā-Allāh (if Allāh ﷺ wills) before we carry out an action, we fulfil our duty in acknowledging that there is a greater power than that of our will at work.

Many of us make firm intentions and take little heed of the fact that it is only through Allāh's ﷺ will that our intentions can be fulfilled. It is when the plan we constructed despite our great effort and preparation does not materialise that we are then compelled to ponder over the forces at work in recognition that there is a will which is greater than that of our will.

This is what compelled Sayyidunā Alī ؓ to say, "I have recognised my Lord through my strong intention breaking. This is because if there is no Creator, then I should be able to do anything I want. But my full intention to carry out an act and then my inability to see it through shows that there is a Creator Who is doing all of this."

An incident occurred during the Prophet's ﷺ lifetime which shows the importance of these words. On one occasion, the disbelievers had consulted with the Jews as to how they would go about finding out if the Prophet ﷺ was indeed a true Prophet. The Jewish rabbis advised them to go to the Prophet ﷺ and ask him three questions. If he was able to answer them, then he was indeed a true Prophet. They advised them to ask the following three questions:
1. Who were the Ashābul kahf (people of the cave)?
2. What is the Rūh (spirit)?
3. Who was Dhul Qarnayn?

The Prophet ﷺ did not recall to say the words *Inshā-Allāh* (if Allāh ﷻ wills) after explaining to the people that he would inform them of the answers the next day. As he waited patiently for revelation to descend to reveal the answers to these questions, the revelation halted. This led to the disbelievers mocking and ridiculing the Prophet ﷺ as he waited anxiously for the answers. According to one Tafsīr, 40 days lapsed before the Prophet ﷺ received the responses to these questions in the form of divine revelation.

This caused great grief to the Prophet ﷺ. When Jibrīl عليه السلام finally descended with the revelation, the first words to be revealed were:

وَلَا تَقُولَنَّ لِشَاْىْ ءٍ إِنِّي فَاعِلٌ ذَٰلِكَ غَدًا ﴿٢٣﴾ إِلَّا أَن يَشَاءَ اللَّهُ وَاذْكُر رَّبَّكَ إِذَا نَسِيتَ وَقُلْ
عَسَىٰ أَن يَهْدِيَنِ رَبِّي لِأَقْرَبَ مِنْ هَٰذَا رَشَدًا ﴿٢٤﴾

**"And never say of anything, 'Indeed, I will do that tomorrow,
Except (when adding), if Allāh wills.' And remember your Lord
when you forget (it) and say, 'Perhaps my Lord will guide me to
what is nearer to this in right conduct.'" (18:23-24)**

Even though they were very simple and straightforward words to recite, the effect of their absence proved critical. This verse reminds us
of the great importance and significance of saying the words Inshā-
Allāh (if Allāh ﷻ wills). By neglecting the importance of reciting
these words, a person deprives themselves of blessings and this only
opens up the door to adverse consequences.

Similar to the story of a man who once went to the market place to
buy a cow. As he was proceeding, he was stopped by a man who
asked, "Where are you going?" He replied, "I am going to the market
to buy a cow." The man who was listening immediately reminded
him to say *Inshā Allāh*. The other man refused to do so, saying that
he had his money in his pocket and the cows were on sale in the
market, so he did not feel the need to say so.

As he proceeded to the market, he was attacked by a gang of robbers
who stole all his money. On the way back home, he met the same
friend who noticed that he had not purchased a cow and asked,
"What happened, where is the cow?" The man replied, "Inshā-Allāh I
went forward, Inshā-Allāh the thief came, Inshā-Allāh, they stole my

money and Inshā-Allāh I am coming back!"

Now all the *Inshā-Allāh* phrases were being blurted out in all the wrong places! Nowadays, instead of using this phrase in its proper manner, we make use of it in an abusive way to the extent that, using this phrase for many has become a trouble-free way of getting out of something which they had not intended to carry out in the first instance.

Even the Ya'jūj and Ma'jūj tribes, whom will be unleashed onto the earth towards the end of time will use the word Inshā-Allāh as they try to scale and dig through the wall which separates them from us. This will in effect, give them the power to penetrate through the wall which Dhul Qarnayn had built to protect the people from them.

Everything can only take place with the will and decree of Allāh ﷻ. By reciting the words *Inshā-Allāh,* we affirm our commitment to the knowledge that nothing can take place except by the will of Allāh ﷻ.

Promised Victory

The verse after mentioning the necessity of reciting, *"Inshā-Allāh"* speaks about the believers who would perform the Umrah and then in accordance with the rites of Umrah, shave or trim their hair. This is a requirement for a Hajj or Umrah to be accepted.

The Messenger of Allāh 鑖 prayed for those that shaved their head three times and once for those who trimmed their hair. This indicates that shaving the head (for men) is more virtuous as opposed to only trimming it.

Six months prior, the Quraysh had amassed all its forces in an attempt to crush the Muslims. It was the strategic plan of digging the trench at the Battle of Khandaq which gave an advantage to the believers to such an extent that it forced the disbelievers to abscond and flee from the battlefield after numerous failed attempts at crossing the trench. This is what led to the victory of the Muslims despite them being outnumbered.

Now they had returned to Makkah Mukarramah into what the disbelievers thought was an open grave, as they had come to perform Umrah and had not brought any arms to protect themselves. This would have had a manifold affect on the disbelievers.

On the one hand, they would have felt that it would have been the perfect time for revenge in annihilating them once and for all but at the same time, they secretly marvelled at the sheer strength and conviction of the believer's faith. To come out like this in full exposure with the threat of pending doom and yet remaining firm in one's belief that Allāh 鑖 would protect them. What kind of resolute force were they fighting? This is the question the disbelievers would have certainly asked themselves as never would they have ever witnessed such determined resolve and unwavering commitment.

This bravery had a profound effect on the disbelievers, which also contributed to tilting the scales in recognising Islām as the truth. The disbelievers realised that there had to be something far greater that compelled the believers to risk their lives to such a degree and level. Although this left an impression on the minds of the disbelievers, nevertheless, they still felt that they had to protect their honour and to allow the Muslims to enter into the holy vicinity without putting up resistance would have signified humiliation in their eyes. This in turn, concluded with the result of a peace treaty being drawn up, which indirectly gave them the status of a force to be reckoned with and ultimately paved the way for the conquest of Makkah Mukarramah.

We have to view success through the lens of the Qur'ān and Hadīth. Many times, victory may not be so apparent. This was the predominant feeling amongst the Sahābah ☙ when the peace treaty of Hudaybiyah was being concluded. The wisdom behind it was not clearly visible or understood immediately.

Artificial Success

In this worldly life, success is often equated to a person's wealth and social standing. In the Qur'ān, Allāh ﷻ informs of the great treasures and riches of Qārūn. People would gasp and marvel at the sight of his wealth.

فَخَرَجَ عَلَىٰ قَوۡمِهِ فِى زِينَتِهِۦ قَالَ الَّذِيۡنَ يُرِيۡدُوۡنَ الۡحَيٰوةَ الدُّنۡيَا يٰلَيۡتَ لَنَا مِثۡلَ مَآ أُوۡتِىَ

Artificial Success

قَٰرُوۡنَ إِنَّهُۥ لَذُو حَظٍّ عَظِيمٍ

"So he came out before his people in his adornment. Those who desired the worldly life said, "Oh, would that we had like what was given to Qārūn. Indeed, he is one of great fortune." (28:79)

Nevertheless, even this enormous amount of wealth that he had amassed could not save him from Allāh's ﷻ wrath and punishment which was sent as he met his end.

فَخَسَفْنَا بِهِ وَبِدَارِهِ الْأَرْضَ فَمَا كَانَ لَهُۥ مِن فِئَةٍ يَنصُرُونَهُۥ مِن دُونِ اللهِ وَمَا كَانَ مِنَ الْمُنتَصِرِينَ

"And We caused the earth to swallow him and his home. And for him there was no company to aid him other than Allāh, nor was he of those who (could) defend themselves." (28:81)

Allāh ﷻ mentions this to serve as a lesson and a reminder to take heed and amend one's conduct before the day comes when it will be too late.

In the time of Sayyidunā Mūsā, Fir'awn (Pharaoh) was the tyrant ruler who exercised ultimate power and authority, controlling the people within his power for 400 years. However, in the end when he was about to drown and saw the clear signs, he declared his belief but by then it was too late. The incident is mentioned in the following verses:

وَجَاوَزْنَا بِبَنِيٓ إِسْرَآئِيلَ الْبَحْرَ فَأَتْبَعَهُمْ فِرْعَوْنُ وَجُنُودُهُۥ بَغْيًا وَعَدْوًا حَتَّىٰٓ إِذَآ أَدْرَكَهُ الْغَرَقُ

قَالَ اٰمَنْتُ أَنَّهُ لَا إِلٰهَ إِلَّا الَّذِىْ اٰمَنَتْ بِهِ بَنُوْٓا إِسْرَآئِيْلَ وَأَنَا مِنَ الْمُسْلِمِيْنَ ﴿٩٠﴾ اٰلْـٰنَ وَقَدْ عَصَيْتَ قَبْلُ وَكُنْتَ مِنَ الْمُفْسِدِيْنَ ﴿٩١﴾ فَالْيَوْمَ نُنَجِّيْكَ بِبَدَنِكَ لِتَكُوْنَ لِمَنْ خَلْفَكَ اٰيَةً وَإِنَّ كَثِيْرًا مِّنَ النَّاسِ عَنْ اٰيٰتِنَا لَغَافِلُوْنَ ﴿٩٢﴾

"And We took the Children of Isrāīl across the sea, and Pharaoh and his soldiers pursued them in tyranny and enmity until when drowning overtook him he said, 'I believe that there is no deity except that in whom the Children of Isrāīl believe, and I am of the Muslims.' 'Now? And you had disobeyed (him) before and were of the corrupters.' So today, We will save you in body so that you may be to those who succeed you a sign. And indeed, many among the people, of Our signs are heedless." (10:90-92)

At the time of death a person will see the Angel of death, but it will be too late to change anything as the doors to repentance will be closed by then.

Acceptance of Du'ās (Supplications)

Sincere Du'ās are accepted but this does not necessitate an immediate result. An example of this is when Sayyidunā Mūsā ﷺ made a Du'ā against Fir'awn (Pharaoh) after he transgressed all bounds of disbelief and disobedience:

وَقَالَ مُوْسٰى رَبَّنَآ إِنَّكَ اٰتَيْتَ فِرْعَوْنَ وَمَلَأَهُ زِيْنَةً وَأَمْوَالًا فِي الْحَيٰوةِ الدُّنْيَا رَبَّنَا لِيُضِلُّوْا عَنْ

127

سَبِيلِكَ ' رَبَّنَا اطْمِسْ عَلَى أَمْوَالِهِمْ وَاشْدُدْ عَلَى قُلُوبِهِمْ فَلَا يُؤْمِنُوا حَتَّى يَرَوُا الْعَذَابَ
الْأَلِيْمَ

**"And Mūsā said, 'Our Lord, indeed You have given Pharaoh and
his establishment splendour and wealth in the worldly life, our
Lord, that they may lead (men) astray from Your way. Our Lord,
obliterate their wealth and harden their hearts so that they will
not believe until they see the painful punishment." (10:88)**

Allāh ﷻ replied to Sayyidunā Mūsā's عليه السلام Du'ā that it had already
been granted. However, the resulting effect of this Du'ā was not seen
until after 40 years later when Fir'awn was drowned.

One can only imagine the sheer level of distress and suffering Sayyidunā Mūsā عليه السلام tolerated and endured in the interim. He preached
for so many years only to be acknowledged partly by Banū Isrāīl.
However, Pharaoh and his followers had crossed all sense of boundaries and limitations; to the point of no return, which compelled Sayyidunā Mūsā عليه السلام to take this severe and extreme measure.

Glad Tidings to the Believers

The believers had reached such a level that they were honoured with
receiving the glad tidings of entering Makkah Mukarramah in order
to perform Umrah. This revelation reinforced motivation in the believers and instilled within them the inner strength to push forward
when things did not quite work out according to their level of expec-

tation. They clung onto the conviction and belief that something far greater lay ahead in wait for them. This was also a distinguishing criterion which separated the true believers from those who had sinister and undisclosed motives concealed in their hearts. Some even started to doubt as to whether or not the Prophet ﷺ did indeed have the dream of performing Umrah with the believers.

These doubts of uncertainty and hesitation were laid to rest when the Prophet's ﷺ vision came to pass. Not only did the whole of Arabia become swept under the tide of Islām within a very short period, but the Message became triumphant and victorious in the hearts and minds of the masses.

هُوَ الَّذِيٓ أَرْسَلَ رَسُولَهُۥ بِالْهُدَىٰ وَدِينِ الْحَقِّ لِيُظْهِرَهُۥ عَلَى الدِّينِ كُلِّهِۦ ۚ وَكَفَىٰ بِٱللَّهِ شَهِيدًا

"It is He Who sent His Messenger with guidance and the religion of truth to manifest it over all religion. And sufficient is Allāh as witness." (48:28)

A new dawning era was being presented before humanity. One of a new faith which had been passed down through the generations; the message being conveyed through the chain of Prophethood until it was revealed to the last and final Messenger of Allāh; our beloved Prophet Muhammad ﷺ, to continue and endure until the end of time.

Despite the Treaty of Hudaybiyah being one-sided and unjust in favouring the polytheists, Allāh ﷻ revealed this verse as an assurance that try as the disbelievers may, imminent success was impending on the horizon for the believers.

Imagine the scene at the time when the verse was revealed with the believers listening on as the Prophet ﷺ recited the revelation that this Message would not only spread, but would eventually become the most dominant religion on the surface of the earth. No other religion has ever made this claim that it was here to stay. There have been many religions which over time have become abolished and wiped out.

One Message, One God

As Muslims, we believe that the Message revealed to mankind was one; to believe and worship in the one true God. Allāh ﷻ sent Prophets and Messengers to instruct the people of this but over time, the message suffered from change and alteration. This led to further Prophets being sent to remind the people of the one true Lord. The difference between the past and present nations is that in the past, Allāh ﷻ sent Prophets to a particular nation or tribe, whereas the Prophet Muhammad ﷺ was assigned as the Final Prophet and Messenger and was sent to the whole of mankind.

Every other book revealed was specific to a particular tribe or civilisation and this is evident when reading other religious holy books. The Qur'ān is the only holy book which makes the claim that, not only is it here to remain permanently until the end of time, but it is for the whole of humankind.

We see throughout history the number of Muslims exponentially rising and a study conducted by the Pew Research Centre found that Islām is the fastest growing religion which is set to become the largest religion in the world by 2070.

To imagine that an unlettered man in the middle of the Arabian desert with a handful of followers could make a prediction that the message he was preaching would one day become the most dominant religion on the surface of this earth, and then for this realisation to materialise, is certainly worthy of serious scrutiny and investigation for any astute observer. The verse continues in saying that Allāh ﷻ is a Witness. The Prophet ﷺ and his Companions ﷺ left this earth before they could see the fulfilment of this vision in terms of dominance in the number of believers, so Allāh ﷻ took it upon Himself to testify that this prophecy would indeed come to fruition and He bore witness to this. Allah ﷻ fulfilled this prophecy in terms of evidence in the latter part of the Prophet's ﷺ life and during the reign of Sayyidunā Umar ﷺ.

Statistics provide proof that we are not far from the fulfilment of this vision in terms of the number of Muslims. To think that there is a possibility that even we may witness this day in our lifetime is awe-inspiring and incredible in itself.

Every other book revealed was for a specific tribe or nation and we see that as the followers died, the religion too dwindled and disappeared because over the course of time, it becomes changed and altered to what it was founded upon. What makes Islām stand out from all other religions is the fact that it was not just sent for a certain segment or community or to serve a specific nation or time period, but as a mercy to the entire humankind and until the end of time. This is what we are indeed witnessing today with Islām becoming the fastest-growing religion in the world and only in a few decades it is set to overtake Christianity to become the largest religion Inshā-Allāh.

Glory of Islām and Zakāt

In terms of its glory and peak of its civilisation, during the time of Sayyidunā Umar Ibn Abdul Azīz ﷺ it remains unsurpassed. The people of that time had become so affluent that there was barely a person to accept Zakāt. It was said that if a person was asked to accept the Zakāt, they would be heard replying, "If you had come yesterday I would have been in need but today I have no need for it." In other words, all their monetary needs had been taken care of and fulfilled. Allāh ﷻ has ordered that the poor have a right to 2.5% of the wealth of the rich and if this was to be acted upon and dispersed, not a single person would remain in poverty.

In today's society, many are not aware of the sheer magnitude of the gap of inequality that exists between the rich and poor. It is incredible and almost inconceivable to think that the richest 62 people in the world own as much wealth as 50% of the entire world's population. There are 195 countries in the world and if wealth was divided equally, it is similar to saying that these 62 people own the equivalent of 97 of the worlds countries wealth. The figures continue to get startling when the realisation dawns that only 1% of the world's population owns 99% of the world's wealth.

In simple terms, it is similar to saying that in every 100 people one person will owe 99 pounds while the other one pound is left to be shared between 99 people. This is the effect of the world's economic system in place today. It certainly does not take great intelligence to recognise that there is something greatly flawed with our economic climate when it generates inequality to this sheer colossal level. No one in their right mind would deny that there is something seriously flawed with a system which allows something of such great disproportionate measures to amass and accumulate. Who is responsible for the situation when a person can amass wealth unconditionally and have no accountability when the wealth they possess in reality would suffice for a million lifetimes. One could even see the injustice and inhumanity that arises from this which allows such a climate to flourish.

We live in a society where we are made to believe that everything we earn is exclusively ours to keep. This is an effect of living in a capitalist global economy. From the Islamic perspective, a person is not denied ownership and can own things which are acquired through effort and skill. Islām only stipulates that a mere 2.5% from a person's annual wealth needs to be given to the destitute. Thereafter, it is permitted for one to do as they please with the rest of their wealth.

In order to avoid excessive build-up of wealth in the hands of a few to the detriment of many is what Islām is opposed to. This is why rules and regulations have been set to ensure that no one is left struggling to get their basic needs and necessities.

If we were to implement this practice in the global economy, then Inshā-Allāh, we would see the success and positive impact that this would have in eradicating poverty. To know that the Qur'ān provided the perfect solution to this problem 1400 years ago is truly extraordinary.

Addressing the Holy Prophet ﷺ

When Allāh ﷻ speaks about the Prophet ﷺ, He addresses him with respective titles of honour. This illustrates his elevated status and merit and serves as a lesson to those around him about how they should address him. Allāh ﷻ says:

$$ لَا تَجْعَلُوا دُعَآءَ الرَّسُولِ بَيْنَكُمْ كَدُعَآءِ بَعْضِكُمْ بَعْضًا $$

"Do not make (your) calling of the Messenger among yourselves as the call of one of you to another. (24:63)"

134

In another place, Allāh ﷻ mentions:

يَـٰٓأَيُّهَا الَّذِينَ ءَامَنُوا لَا تَرْفَعُوٓا أَصْوَٰتَكُمْ فَوْقَ صَوْتِ النَّبِيِّ وَلَا تَجْهَرُوا لَهُۥ بِالْقَوْلِ كَجَهْرِ بَعْضِكُمْ لِبَعْضٍ أَن تَحْبَطَ أَعْمَٰلُكُمْ وَأَنتُمْ لَا تَشْعُرُونَ ﴿٢﴾ إِنَّ الَّذِينَ يَغُضُّونَ أَصْوَٰتَهُمْ عِندَ رَسُولِ اللَّهِ أُوْلَٰٓئِكَ الَّذِينَ امْتَحَنَ اللَّهُ قُلُوبَهُمْ لِلتَّقْوَىٰ لَهُم مَّغْفِرَةٌ وَأَجْرٌ عَظِيمٌ ﴿٣﴾

"O you who have believed, do not raise your voices above the voice of the Prophet or be loud to him in speech like the loudness of some of you to others, lest your deeds become worthless while you perceive not. Indeed, those who lower their voices before the Messenger of Allāh - they are the ones whose hearts Allāh has tested for righteousness. For them is forgiveness and great reward." (49:2-3)

Allāh ﷻ refrains from addressing him by his name except in exceptional circumstances. One such instance of this was when the Quraysh were drawing up the terms and conditions of the Treaty of Hudaybiyah. Sayyidunā Alī ؓ had written, 'The Messenger of Allāh agrees...' whereupon the Quraysh became defiant and said to write, 'Muhammad, the son of Abdullāh agrees...'

They proclaimed that since they did not believe him to be the Messenger of Allāh, how then could they allow it to be written in the Treaty? The believers became enraged by this incident. However, the Prophet ﷺ agreed to their terms and with his blessed hands erased the portion which read 'the Messenger of Allāh' as Sayyidunā Alī ؓ, owing to the great love for the Prophet ﷺ refused to wipe it out. It was in direct response to this that Allāh ﷻ revealed the following verse:

مُحَمَّدٌ رَّسُوْلُ اللهِ ۚ وَالَّذِيْنَ مَعَهٗ أَشِدَّآءُ عَلَى الْكُفَّارِ رُحَمَآءُ بَيْنَهُمْ

Muhammad is the Messenger of Allāh, and those with him are stern against the disbelievers, merciful among themselves.
(48:29)

It was to reaffirm that Prophet ﷺ was indeed the Messenger of Allāh ﷻ. The verse is proclaiming that, did the disbelievers think that they could conceal the fact that the Prophet Muhammad ﷺ was the Messenger of Allāh by having this recognition erased from the treaty? Did they think that through their actions, his living memory would be erased and would be forgotten forever?

Allāh ﷻ responds by declaring that as much as they may conspire against him and not only is he the Messenger of Allāh but his Message would also become dominant and flourish to all the corners of the earth, as we are indeed witnessing today. They may have succeeded in wiping out the Prophet's ﷺ name off the treaty, but Allāh ﷻ would preserve his name forever in the Holy Qur'ān, for all times and generations to come.

Allāh ﷻ directly mentions the Prophet ﷺ by name on only four occasions which were to directly address and clear misconceptions held by the disbelievers.

Verse 29 from Sūrah Al-Fath has already been mentioned where Allāh ﷻ addresses the Prophet ﷺ by his name. The second time his name has been mentioned was after the Battle of Uhud took place where rumours spread that he had been martyred. These doubts were quickly expelled and laid to rest when Allāh ﷻ revealed the following verse:

وَمَا مُحَمَّدٌ إِلَّا رَسُولٌ قَدْ خَلَتْ مِنْ قَبْلِهِ الرُّسُلُ أَفَإِنْ مَّاتَ أَوْ قُتِلَ انْقَلَبْتُمْ عَلَى أَعْقَابِكُمْ وَمَنْ يَنْقَلِبْ عَلَى عَقِبَيْهِ فَلَنْ يَّضُرَّ اللهَ شَيْئًا وَسَيَجْزِى اللهُ الشَّاكِرِينَ

"Muhammad is not but a Messenger. (Other) Messengers have passed on before him. So if he was to die or be killed, would you turn back on your heels (to disbelief)? And he who turns back on his heels will never harm Allāh at all, but Allāh will reward the grateful." (3:144)

The third place his name is mentioned is in Sūrah Al-Ahzāb.

مَّا كَانَ مُحَمَّدٌ أَبَآ أَحَدٍ مِّنْ رِّجَالِكُمْ وَلَٰكِنْ رَّسُولَ اللهِ وَخَاتَمَ ٱلنَّبِيِّنَ وَكَانَ اللهُ بِكُلِّ شَىْءٍ عَلِيمًا

"Muhammad is not the father of (any) one of you men but (he is) the Messenger of Allāh and last of the Prophets. And ever is Allāh of all things, Knowing. (33:40)

A person was always to be addressed by attributing the name of their biological father to avoid any confusion arising in the future. Before the advent of Islām, the Prophet ﷺ had adopted Zaid Ibn Hāritha ؓ who was known as Zaid Ibn Muhammad. Allāh ﷻ revealed this verse to clear up any misconceptions amongst the people that he was the Prophet's ﷺ biological son.

The fourth place where Allāh ﷻ mentioned his name was to reaffirm that he was the one who was chosen to be given the Message and hence the necessity to mention him by name:

$$وَالَّذِيْنَ اٰمَنُوْا وَعَمِلُوا الصّٰلِحٰتِ وَاٰمَنُوْا بِمَا نُزِّلَ عَلٰى مُحَمَّدٍ وَّهُوَ الْحَقُّ مِنْ رَّبِّهِمْ كَفَّرَ عَنْهُمْ سَيِّاٰتِهِمْ وَاَصْلَحَ بَالَهُمْ$$

"And those who believe and do righteous deeds and believe what has been sent down upon Muhammad and it is the truth from their Lord, He will remove from them their misdeeds and amend their condition. (47:2)

On one occasion, the Prophet ﷺ was referred to as Ahmad:

$$وَإِذْ قَالَ عِيْسَى ابْنُ مَرْيَمَ يٰبَنِيْ إِسْرَآئِيْلَ إِنِّيْ رَسُوْلُ اللّٰهِ إِلَيْكُمْ مُّصَدِّقًا لِّمَا بَيْنَ يَدَيَّ مِنَ التَّوْرٰةِ وَمُبَشِّرًۢا بِرَسُوْلٍ يَّأْتِيْ مِنْۢ بَعْدِى اسْمُهٗ أَحْمَدُ فَلَمَّا جَآءَهُمْ بِالْبَيِّنٰتِ قَالُوْا هٰذَا سِحْرٌ مُّبِيْنٌ$$

"And (mention) when Īsā, son of Maryam said, 'O children of Isrāīl, indeed I am the Messenger of Allāh to you confirming what came before me of the Tawrāh and bringing good tidings of a Messenger to come after me, whose name is Ahmad.' But when

138

he came to them with clear evidences, they said, 'This is obvious magic.' (61:6)

As much as the disbelievers persisted in turning the believers away from Islām; they failed. Allāh ﷻ reminds them that try as they may, they will not succeed.

وَمَن يَبْتَغِ غَيْرَ الْإِسْلَٰمِ دِينًا فَلَن يُقْبَلَ مِنْهُ وَهُوَ فِي الْأَخِرَةِ مِنَ الْخَٰسِرِينَ

"And whoever desires other than Islām as religion, never will it be accepted from him, and he, in the Hereafter will be among the losers." (3:85)

Muhammad ﷺ was the seal of all the Prophets ﷺ and he came with the last and complete revelation given to man. Therefore, no other religion is acceptable. For those that fail to recognise it as valid and correct, will come to acknowledge and confess to its truth at the moment when death will strike them, but by then it will be too late.

Misjudgements Addressed

In addition to the above, Allāh ﷻ has addressed the Prophet ﷺ for misjudgements. We have to remember that Allāh ﷻ had already declared forgiveness for him as previously mentioned with regards to rewards that were given to the Prophet ﷺ.

On one occasion, the hypocrites came to the Prophet ﷺ and put forward their excuses to avoid going out to fight to defend the Muslims. The Prophet ﷺ accepted their explanations and excused them from fighting. He was addressed by Allāh ﷻ as it was not clear who the truthful and genuine ones were from the untruthful and misguided ones.

On another occasion the Prophet ﷺ was caused to draw away from a blind Sahābi because he was busy addressing some other people. Regarding this, Allāh ﷻ reproached the Prophet ﷺ as to how he should have approached the blind Sahābi, Sayyidunā Abdullāh Ibn Umme Makhtūm ؓ; in addressing his immediate needs even though he was busy conversing with the chiefs of Makkah Mukarramah who had gathered.

Momentarily being focused on the chiefs, his attention was diverted, and as a result, he turned himself away from the blind Sahābi ؓ who had come with such eagerness. Immediately, Allāh ﷻ revealed the following verses in correcting the Prophet ﷺ that this was unbefitting for the Prophet ﷺ to behave in this manner, giving preference to the chiefs in calling them to Islām even though they showed no interest in contemplating the message. This is stated in the following verses:

عَبَسَ وَتَوَلّٰى ﴿١﴾ اَنْ جَآءَهُ الْاَعْمٰى ﴿٢﴾ وَمَا يُدْرِيْكَ لَعَلَّهٗ يَزَّكّٰى ﴿٣﴾ اَوْ يَذَّكَّرُ فَتَنْفَعَهُ الذِّكْرٰى ﴿٤﴾ اَمَّا مَنِ اسْتَغْنٰى ﴿٥﴾ فَاَنْتَ لَهٗ تَصَدّٰى ﴿٦﴾ وَمَا عَلَيْكَ اَلَّا يَزَّكّٰى ﴿٧﴾ وَاَمَّا مَنْ جَآءَكَ يَسْعٰى ﴿٨﴾ وَهُوَ يَخْشٰى ﴿٩﴾ فَاَنْتَ عَنْهُ تَلَهّٰى ﴿١٠﴾

"The Prophet frowned and turned away because there came to him the blind man (interrupting). But what would make you perceive (O Muhammad), that perhaps he might be purified? Or be reminded and the remembrance would benefit him? As for he who thinks of himself without need, to him, you give attention. And not upon you (is any blame) if he will not be purified. But as for he who came to you striving (for knowledge), while he fears (Allāh), from him you are distracted." (80:1-10)

Concluding Verse of Sūrah Al-Fath

مُحَمَّدٌ رَّسُوْلُ اللهِ وَالَّذِيْنَ مَعَهُ أَشِدَّآءُ عَلَى الْكُفَّارِ رُحَمَآءُ بَيْنَهُمْ تَرٰىهُمْ رُكَّعًا سُجَّدًا يَّبْتَغُوْنَ فَضْلًا مِّنَ اللهِ وَرِضْوَانًا سِيْمَاهُمْ فِيْ وُجُوْهِهِمْ مِّنْ أَثَرِ السُّجُوْدِ ذٰلِكَ مَثَلُهُمْ فِي التَّوْرٰىةِ وَمَثَلُهُمْ فِي الْإِنْجِيْلِ كَزَرْعٍ أَخْرَجَ شَطْأَهُ فَأٰزَرَهُ فَاسْتَغْلَظَ فَاسْتَوٰى عَلٰى سُوْقِهِ يُعْجِبُ الزُّرَّاعَ لِيَغِيْظَ بِهِمُ الْكُفَّارَ وَعَدَ اللهُ الَّذِيْنَ اٰمَنُوْا وَعَمِلُوا الصّٰلِحٰتِ مِنْهُمْ مَّغْفِرَةً وَّأَجْرًا عَظِيْمًا

"Muhammad is the Messenger of Allāh and those with him are stern against the disbelievers, merciful among themselves. You see them bowing and prostrating, (in prayer) seeking bounty from Allāh and (His) pleasure. Their mark is on their faces from the trace of prostration. That is their description in the Tawrāh. And their description in the Bible is as a plant which produces its offshoots and strengthens them so they grow firm and stand upon their stalks, delighting the sowers so that Allāh may enrage

by them the disbelievers. Allāh has promised those who believe and do righteous deeds among them forgiveness and a great reward." (48:29)

The last verse of this Sūrah begins by describing the qualities and virtues of the Sahābah ﷺ. During the times of battles when defending the Prophet ﷺ, in spite of the greatest adverse and unfavourable conditions, the Sahābah ﷺ stood firm and resilient. They endured pain and hardship while remaining resolute and determined; unwavering in their support and commitment to the Prophet ﷺ. They displayed steadfastness in their loyalty and support of the Prophet ﷺ.

Even during times when they were faced with conflicting concepts and views which appeared to contradict their own opinions, they placed their trust in the Prophet ﷺ, believing that his decisions and course of action would lead to success and gain the most favourable outcome. This is indeed what we witness after the Treaty of Hudaybiyah which was followed by a rapid growth of the Muslims over the next two years and eventually the conquest of Makkah Mukarramah. Allāh ﷻ describes the virtues of the Sahābah ﷺ. He recounts and sets out the deeds which they were found to most engage in. Owing to their prolonged prostration, they would often be left with the mark of prostration on their forehead, which is described in the Tawrāh.

Hasan Al-Basri ﷺ describes a person who performs the Tahajjud prayer, that they will have Nūr on their face and will cross the bridge

(Sirāt) like the speed of lightning. In the Gospel, they are resembled with the likeness of plants; growing from seeds; strong and firm thus infuriating the disbelievers.

When the Prophet ﷺ proclaimed the message of Islām, the first woman to accept the call was his wife Sayyidah Khadījah ﵂. The first man who responded to the message was Sayyidunā Abū Bakr ﵁. The first child who accepted Islām was Sayyidunā Alī ﵁ whilst the first slave was Sayyidunā Zaid Ibn Hāritha ﵁.

Sayyidunā Umar ﵁ was the fortieth person to enter into Islām and it was at that point Allāh ﷻ revealed that the number of Muslims had become sufficient.

يَٰٓأَيُّهَا النَّبِيُّ حَسْبُكَ اللهُ وَمَنِ اتَّبَعَكَ مِنَ الْمُؤْمِنِينَ

"O Prophet, sufficient for you is Allāh and whoever follows you of the believers." (8:64)

Up until the point of Sayyidunā Umar's ﵁ conversion, the believers could not pray their Salāh openly because of being attacked. It was only after Sayyidunā Umar's ﵁ conversion that he and Sayyidunā Hamzah ﵁ (the Prophet's ﷺ uncle) would stand at each end of the row while the believers prayed in front of the Holy Ka'bah.

Deviant Beliefs about the Sahābah ﷺ

There are some who hold incorrect beliefs, discrediting and maligning the Sahābah ﷺ. Not only do they search for faults, but they actively engage in slandering the Prophet's ﷺ Companions ﷺ. Regarding this Sayyidunā Abū Sa'īd Al-Khudrī ﷺ reported that Allāh's Messenger ﷺ said, "Do not curse my Companions! Do not curse my Companions! I swear by Him in Whose hand my life is, that even if one among you had as much gold as mount Uhud and spent it in the way of Allāh, this would not be equal in reward to a handful spent by them or even to its half."

Imām Tirmidhī ﷺ and Imām Ibn Hibbān ﷺ quote from Sayyidunā Abdullāh Ibn Mughaffal ﷺ that Allāh's Messenger ﷺ said, "Fear Allāh; fear Allāh and (refrain from using bad language) about my Companions! (He said it twice). Do not make them the target of your attacks after me! Whoever loves them, loves them on account of his love for me; whoever hates them, hates them on account of his hate for me. He who maligns them, has maligned me and he who maligns me has maligned Allāh and it is very soon that Allāh punishes those who malign Him."

The Sahābah ﷺ are above criticism because Allāh ﷻ has mentioned in the Qur'ān that He is pleased with them as well as them being pleased with Him. They were also given the glad tidings of entering Paradise. They renounced the pleasures of the world, sacrificing their wealth and their lives; forgoing their own safety and comfort in defending the Prophet ﷺ in spreading the Dīn of Islām.

The torment and hardship they encountered; they bore with steadfastness and loyalty. The suffering and struggles they endured were necessary for having earned them the right to be above being criticised or being spoken about in an unpleasant or negative manner.

Sayyidunā Abdullāh Ibn Mas'ūd ﷺ narrates that the Holy Prophet ﷺ said, "The best of the people are my generation, then those who come after them, then those who come after them." (Bukhāri, Muslim)

The love the Prophet ﷺ had for the Sahābah ﷺ was as a result of their devotion and commitment to him. Allāh ﷺ safeguarded them from going on the wrong path.

Not withstanding this, there are still some who go to even greater measures of misguidance and deviance, accusing our beloved mother of the believers; Sayyidah 'Āisha ﷺ of adultery. This slander was levelled against her during the time of the Prophet ﷺ but she was cleared of any wrongdoing through the revelation of Sūrah An-Nūr. The Qur'ān also warns against those who level such accusation without any proof or witnesses in the following verses:

$$\text{إِنَّ الَّذِيْنَ يَرْمُوْنَ الْمُحْصَنٰتِ الْغٰفِلٰتِ الْمُؤْمِنٰتِ لُعِنُوْا فِي الدُّنْيَا وَالْاٰخِرَةِ وَلَهُمْ عَذَابٌ عَظِيْمٌ}$$

"Indeed, those who (falsely) accuse chaste, unaware and believing women are cursed in this world and the Hereafter and they will have a great punishment." (24:23)

وَالَّذِينَ يَرْمُونَ الْمُحْصَنَتِ ثُمَّ لَمْ يَأْتُوا بِأَرْبَعَةِ شُهَدَآءَ فَاجْلِدُوهُمْ ثَمَنِينَ جَلْدَةً وَلَا تَقْبَلُوا لَهُمْ شَهَدَةً أَبَدًا ۚ وَأُوْلَئِكَ هُمُ الْفَسِقُونَ ﴿٤﴾ إِلَّا الَّذِينَ تَابُوا مِنْ بَعْدِ ذَلِكَ وَأَصْلَحُوا فَإِنَّ اللهَ غَفُورٌ رَّحِيمٌ ﴿٥﴾

"And those who accuse chaste women and then do not produce four witnesses, lash them with eighty lashes and do not accept from them testimony ever after and they are defiantly disobedient. Except those who repent thereafter and reform, for indeed Allāh is forgiving and Merciful." (24:4-5)

Those who obey Allāh ﷻ and His Messenger ﷺ, for them will be forgiveness and a rich reward as Allāh ﷻ says in the following verse:

يَا أَيُّهَا الَّذِينَ ءَامَنُوا تُوبُوا إِلَى اللهِ تَوْبَةً نَّصُوحًا عَسَى رَبُّكُمْ أَن يُكَفِّرَ عَنكُمْ سَيِّئَاتِكُمْ وَيُدْخِلَكُمْ جَنَّتٍ تَجْرِي مِنْ تَحْتِهَا الْأَنْهَرُ يَوْمَ لَا يُخْزِى اللهُ النَّبِيَّ وَالَّذِينَ ءَامَنُوا مَعَهُ نُورُهُمْ يَسْعَى بَيْنَ أَيْدِيهِمْ وَبِأَيْمَنِهِمْ يَقُولُونَ رَبَّنَا أَتْمِمْ لَنَا نُورَنَا وَاغْفِرْ لَنَا إِنَّكَ عَلَى كُلِّ شَىْءٍ قَدِيرٌ

"O you who have believed! Repent to Allāh with sincere repentance. Perhaps your Lord will remove from you your misdeeds and admit you into gardens beneath which rivers flow (on) the Day when Allāh will not disgrace the Prophet and those who be-

lieve in him. Their light will proceed before them and on their right; they will say, "Our Lord, perfect for us our light and forgive us. Indeed, You are over all things Competent." (66:8)

Just as the Sahābah 🌸 were given glad tidings before they had departed from this world, owing to their sheer dedication and commitment of making the Dīn of Allāh 🌸 supreme, our pious predecessors who followed in their footsteps were also blessed with fortunate dreams and visions in one form or another as a result of their sacrifices and effort. They abandoned their worldly comfort and pleasures, foregoing their life of luxury and ease for a life of toil and struggle, in recognition of the transitory nature of the life of this Dunya.

Our beloved Prophet 🌸 has given us clear guidance to follow in directing us to the path of success. As human beings, we will inevitably err and commit mistakes, but by turning to Allāh 🌸 in sincere repentance, we have the door to salvation wide open.

May Allāh 🌸 grant us the Tawfīq (ability) to sincerely repent from our wrongdoings and misconduct, and enable us to enter into the doors and realm of His outstretched Mercy. Āmīn.

English Translation of

سورة الفتح
Sūrah 48 Al-Fath
(The Victory)
(Madani | 29 Verses)

Indeed We have given you (O Muhammad) a clear conquest	1	إِنَّا فَتَحْنَا لَكَ فَتْحًا مُّبِينًا ۞
That Allāh may forgive for you what preceded of your sin and what will follow and complete His favour upon you and guide you to a straight path.	2	لِّيَغْفِرَ لَكَ اللَّهُ مَا تَقَدَّمَ مِن ذَنبِكَ وَمَا تَأَخَّرَ وَيُتِمَّ نِعْمَتَهُ عَلَيْكَ وَيَهْدِيَكَ صِرَاطًا مُّسْتَقِيمًا ۞
And (that) Allāh may aid you with a mighty victory.	3	وَيَنصُرَكَ اللَّهُ نَصْرًا عَزِيزًا ۞
It is He Who sent down tranquillity into the hearts of the believers that they would increase in faith along with their (present) faith. And to Allāh belong the soldiers of the heavens and the earth and ever is Allāh Knowing and Wise.	4	هُوَ الَّذِي أَنزَلَ السَّكِينَةَ فِي قُلُوبِ الْمُؤْمِنِينَ لِيَزْدَادُوا إِيمَانًا مَّعَ إِيمَانِهِمْ ۗ وَلِلَّهِ جُنُودُ السَّمَاوَاتِ وَالْأَرْضِ ۚ وَكَانَ اللَّهُ عَلِيمًا حَكِيمًا ۞
(And) that He may admit the believing men and the believing women to gardens beneath which rivers flow to abide therein eternally and remove from them their misdeeds and ever is that, in the sight of Allāh, a great attainment.	5	لِّيُدْخِلَ الْمُؤْمِنِينَ وَالْمُؤْمِنَاتِ جَنَّاتٍ تَجْرِي مِن تَحْتِهَا الْأَنْهَارُ خَالِدِينَ فِيهَا وَيُكَفِّرَ عَنْهُمْ سَيِّئَاتِهِمْ ۚ وَكَانَ ذَٰلِكَ عِندَ اللَّهِ فَوْزًا عَظِيمًا ۞
And (that) He may punish the hypocrite men and hypocrite women, and the polytheist men and polytheist women - those who assume about Allāh an assumption of evil nature. Upon them is a misfortune of evil nature, and Allāh has become angry with them	6	وَيُعَذِّبَ الْمُنَافِقِينَ وَالْمُنَافِقَاتِ وَالْمُشْرِكِينَ وَالْمُشْرِكَاتِ الظَّانِّينَ بِاللَّهِ ظَنَّ السَّوْءِ ۚ عَلَيْهِمْ دَائِرَةُ السَّوْءِ ۖ وَغَضِبَ اللَّهُ عَلَيْهِمْ وَلَعَنَهُمْ وَأَعَدَّ لَهُمْ جَهَنَّمَ ۖ وَسَاءَتْ مَصِيرًا ۞

and has cursed them and prepared for them Hell, and evil it is as the destination.	6	
And to Allāh belongs the soldiers of the heavens and the earth. And ever is Allāh Exalted in Might and Wise.	7	وَلِلّٰهِ جُنُودُ السَّمَاوَاتِ وَالْأَرْضِ ۚ وَكَانَ اللّٰهُ عَزِيزًا حَكِيمًا ۝
Indeed, We have sent you as a witness and a bringer of good tidings and a warner.	8	إِنَّا أَرْسَلْنَاكَ شَاهِدًا وَمُبَشِّرًا وَنَذِيرًا ۝
That you (people) may believe in Allāh and His Messenger and honour him and respect the Prophet and exalt Allāh morning and afternoon.	9	لِتُؤْمِنُوا بِاللّٰهِ وَرَسُولِهِ وَتُعَزِّرُوهُ وَتُوَقِّرُوهُ وَتُسَبِّحُوهُ بُكْرَةً وَأَصِيلًا ۝
Indeed, those who pledge allegiance to you (O Muhammad), they are actually pledging allegiance to Allāh. The hand of Allāh is over their hands. So he who breaks his word, only breaks it to the detriment of himself. And he who fulfils that which he has promised Allāh, He will give him a great reward.	10	إِنَّ الَّذِينَ يُبَايِعُونَكَ إِنَّمَا يُبَايِعُونَ اللّٰهَ يَدُ اللّٰهِ فَوْقَ أَيْدِيهِمْ ۚ فَمَنْ نَّكَثَ فَإِنَّمَا يَنكُثُ عَلَىٰ نَفْسِهِ ۖ وَمَنْ أَوْفَىٰ بِمَا عَاهَدَ عَلَيْهُ اللّٰهَ فَسَيُؤْتِيهِ أَجْرًا عَظِيمًا ۝
Those who remained of the Bedouins will say to you, "Our properties and our families occupied us, so ask forgiveness for us." They say with their tongues what is not within their hearts. Say, "Then who could prevent Allāh at all if He intended for you harm or intended for you benefit? Rather, ever is Allāh with what you do, Acquainted."	11	سَيَقُولُ لَكَ الْمُخَلَّفُونَ مِنَ الْأَعْرَابِ شَغَلَتْنَا أَمْوَالُنَا وَأَهْلُونَا فَاسْتَغْفِرْ لَنَا ۚ يَقُولُونَ بِأَلْسِنَتِهِم مَّا لَيْسَ فِي قُلُوبِهِمْ ۚ قُلْ فَمَن يَمْلِكُ لَكُم مِّنَ اللّٰهِ شَيْئًا إِنْ أَرَادَ بِكُمْ ضَرًّا أَوْ أَرَادَ بِكُمْ نَفْعًا ۚ بَلْ كَانَ اللّٰهُ بِمَا تَعْمَلُونَ خَبِيرًا ۝

But you thought that the Messenger and the believers would never return to their families, ever, and that was made pleasing in your hearts. And you assumed an assumption of evil and became ruined people.	12	بَلْ ظَنَنْتُمْ أَنْ لَنْ يَنْقَلِبَ الرَّسُولُ وَالْمُؤْمِنُونَ إِلَى أَهْلِيهِمْ أَبَدًا وَزُيِّنَ ذَلِكَ فِي قُلُوبِكُمْ وَظَنَنْتُمْ ظَنَّ السَّوْءِ وَكُنْتُمْ قَوْمًا بُورًا ۞
And whoever has not believed in Allāh and His Messenger, then indeed We have prepared for the disbelievers a blaze.	13	وَمَنْ لَمْ يُؤْمِنْ بِاللَّهِ وَرَسُولِهِ فَإِنَّا أَعْتَدْنَا لِلْكَافِرِينَ سَعِيرًا ۞
And to Allāh belongs the dominion of the heavens and the earth. He forgives whom He wills and punishes whom He wills. And ever is Allāh Forgiving and Merciful.	14	وَلِلَّهِ مُلْكُ السَّمَاوَاتِ وَالْأَرْضِ يَغْفِرُ لِمَنْ يَشَاءُ وَيُعَذِّبُ مَنْ يَشَاءُ وَكَانَ اللَّهُ غَفُورًا رَحِيمًا ۞
Those who lagged behind will say when you depart to collect the gains, "Let us follow you." They want to change the Word of Allāh. Say, "You will not follow us; Allāh has said so before." Then they will say, "But you are jealous of us." In fact, they understand only a little.	15	سَيَقُولُ الْمُخَلَّفُونَ إِذَا انْطَلَقْتُمْ إِلَى مَغَانِمَ لِتَأْخُذُوهَا ذَرُونَا نَتَّبِعْكُمْ يُرِيدُونَ أَنْ يُبَدِّلُوا كَلَمَ اللَّهِ قُلْ لَنْ تَتَّبِعُونَا كَذَلِكُمْ قَالَ اللَّهُ مِنْ قَبْلُ فَسَيَقُولُونَ بَلْ تَحْسُدُونَنَا بَلْ كَانُوا لَا يَفْقَهُونَ إِلَّا قَلِيلًا ۞
Say to those who remained behind of the Bedouin, You will be called to (face) people of great military might; you may fight them, or they will submit. So if you obey, Allāh will give you a good reward; if you turn away as you turned away before, He will punish you	16	قُلْ لِلْمُخَلَّفِينَ مِنَ الْأَعْرَابِ سَتُدْعَوْنَ إِلَى قَوْمٍ أُولِي بَأْسٍ شَدِيدٍ تُقَاتِلُونَهُمْ أَوْ يُسْلِمُونَ فَإِنْ تُطِيعُوا يُؤْتِكُمُ اللَّهُ أَجْرًا حَسَنًا وَإِنْ تَتَوَلَّوْا كَمَا تَوَلَّيْتُمْ مِنْ قَبْلُ يُعَذِّبْكُمْ عَذَابًا أَلِيمًا ۞

with a painful punishment.	16	
There is not upon the blind any guilt or upon the lame any guilt or upon the ill any guilt (for remaining behind). And whoever obeys Allāh and His Messenger, He will admit him to gardens beneath which rivers flow, but whoever turns away, He will punish him with a painful punishment.	17	لَيْسَ عَلَى الْأَعْمَى حَرَجٌ وَّلَا عَلَى الْأَعْرَجِ حَرَجٌ وَّلَا عَلَى الْمَرِيضِ حَرَجٌ ۗ وَمَنْ يُّطِعِ اللّٰهَ وَرَسُولَهُ يُدْخِلْهُ جَنَّاتٍ تَجْرِيْ مِنْ تَحْتِهَا الْأَنْهَارُ ۚ وَمَنْ يَّتَوَلَّ يُعَذِّبْهُ عَذَابًا أَلِيْمًا ۞
Certainly Allāh was pleased with the believers when they pledged allegiance to you (O Muhammad) under the tree and He knew what was in their hearts, so He sent down tranquillity upon them and rewarded them with an imminent conquest.	18	لَقَدْ رَضِيَ اللّٰهُ عَنِ الْمُؤْمِنِيْنَ إِذْ يُبَايِعُوْنَكَ تَحْتَ الشَّجَرَةِ فَعَلِمَ مَا فِيْ قُلُوْبِهِمْ فَأَنْزَلَ السَّكِيْنَةَ عَلَيْهِمْ وَأَثَابَهُمْ فَتْحًا قَرِيْبًا ۞
And much war booty which they will take. And ever is Allah Exalted in Might and Wise.	19	وَمَغَانِمَ كَثِيْرَةً يَّأْخُذُوْنَهَا ۗ وَكَانَ اللّٰهُ عَزِيْزًا حَكِيْمًا ۞
Allāh has promised you much booty that you will take (in the future) and has hastened for you this (victory) and withheld the hands of people from you -that it may be a sign for the believers and (that) He may guide you to a straight path.	20	وَعَدَكُمُ اللّٰهُ مَغَانِمَ كَثِيْرَةً تَأْخُذُوْنَهَا فَعَجَّلَ لَكُمْ هٰذِهِ وَكَفَّ أَيْدِيَ النَّاسِ عَنْكُمْ وَلِتَكُوْنَ آيَةً لِّلْمُؤْمِنِيْنَ وَيَهْدِيَكُمْ صِرَاطًا مُّسْتَقِيْمًا ۞
And (He promises) other (victories) that you were (so far) unable to (realise) which Allāh has already encompassed. And ever is Allāh over all things, Competent."	21	وَأُخْرَى لَمْ تَقْدِرُوْا عَلَيْهَا قَدْ أَحَاطَ اللّٰهُ بِهَا وَكَانَ اللّٰهُ عَلَى كُلِّ شَيْءٍ قَدِيْرًا ۞

And if those (Makkans) who disbelieve had fought with you, they would have turned their backs. Then they would not find any protector or a helper.	22	وَلَوْ قُتَلَكُمُ الَّذِيْنَ كَفَرُوا لَوَلَّوُا الْأَدْبَارَ ثُمَّ لَا يَجِدُوْنَ وَلِيًّا وَّلَا نَصِيْرًا ۞
(This is) the established way of Allāh which has occurred before. And never will you find in the way of Allāh any change	23	سُنَّةَ اللهِ الَّتِيْ قَدْ خَلَتْ مِنْ قَبْلُ ۖ وَلَنْ تَجِدَ لِسُنَّةِ اللهِ تَبْدِيْلًا ۞
And it is He Who withheld their hands from you and your hands from them in (the area of) Makkah after He caused you to overcome them. Allāh is always Watchful over what you do.	24	وَهُوَ الَّذِيْ كَفَّ أَيْدِيَهُمْ عَنْكُمْ وَأَيْدِيَكُمْ عَنْهُم بِبَطْنِ مَكَّةَ مِنْ بَعْدِ أَنْ أَظْفَرَكُمْ عَلَيْهِمْ ۚ وَكَانَ اللهُ بِمَا تَعْمَلُوْنَ بَصِيْرًا ۞
They are the ones who disbelieved and obstructed you from Masjid Harām while the sacrificial animals were restrained from reaching its place of sacrifice. And if not for believing men and believing women whom you did not know that you might trample them, and you unknowingly suffer harm on their account, the matter would have been concluded (you would have been permitted to enter Makkah). (This was so) That Allāh might admit to His Mercy whom He willed. If they had been apart (from them), We would have punished those who disbelieved among them with a painful punishment."	25	هُمُ الَّذِيْنَ كَفَرُوا وَصَدُّوْكُمْ عَنِ الْمَسْجِدِ الْحَرَامِ وَالْهَدْيَ مَعْكُوْفًا أَنْ يَّبْلُغَ مَحِلَّهُ ۚ وَلَوْلَا رِجَالٌ مُّؤْمِنُوْنَ وَنِسَاءٌ مُّؤْمِنَاتٌ لَّمْ تَعْلَمُوْهُمْ أَنْ تَطَئُوْهُمْ فَتُصِيْبَكُمْ مِّنْهُمْ مَّعَرَّةٌ بِغَيْرِ عِلْمٍ ۚ لِيُدْخِلَ اللهُ فِيْ رَحْمَتِه مَنْ يَّشَاءُ ۚ لَوْ تَزَيَّلُوْا لَعَذَّبْنَا الَّذِيْنَ كَفَرُوْا مِنْهُمْ عَذَابًا أَلِيْمًا ۞

When those who disbelieved had put into their hearts disdain – the disdain of the time of ignorance. But Allāh sent down His tranquillity upon His Messenger and upon the believers and imposed upon them the Word of righteousness and they were more deserving of it and worthy of it. And ever is Allāh of all things Knowing.	26	إِذْ جَعَلَ الَّذِينَ كَفَرُوا فِي قُلُوبِهِمُ الْحَمِيَّةَ حَمِيَّةَ الْجَاهِلِيَّةِ فَأَنْزَلَ اللَّهُ سَكِينَتَهُ عَلَى رَسُولِهِ وَعَلَى الْمُؤْمِنِينَ وَأَلْزَمَهُمْ كَلِمَةَ التَّقْوَى وَكَانُوا أَحَقَّ بِهَا وَأَهْلَهَا ۚ وَكَانَ اللَّهُ بِكُلِّ شَيْءٍ عَلِيمًا ۞
Certainly has Allāh showed to His Messenger the vision in truth. You will surely enter Masjid Harām if Allāh wills in safety, with your heads shaved and (hair) shortened, not fearing (anyone). He knew what you did not know and has arranged before that a conquest near (at hand).	27	لَقَدْ صَدَقَ اللَّهُ رَسُولَهُ الرُّؤْيَا بِالْحَقِّ لَتَدْخُلُنَّ الْمَسْجِدَ الْحَرَامَ إِنْ شَاءَ اللَّهُ آمِنِينَ مُحَلِّقِينَ رُءُوسَكُمْ وَمُقَصِّرِينَ لَا تَخَافُونَ ۖ فَعَلِمَ مَا لَمْ تَعْلَمُوا فَجَعَلَ مِنْ دُونِ ذَلِكَ فَتْحًا قَرِيبًا ۞
It is He Who sent His Messenger with guidance and the religion of truth to manifest it over all religion. And sufficient is Allāh as witness.	28	هُوَ الَّذِي أَرْسَلَ رَسُولَهُ بِالْهُدَى وَدِينِ الْحَقِّ لِيُظْهِرَهُ عَلَى الدِّينِ كُلِّهِ ۚ وَكَفَى بِاللَّهِ شَهِيدًا ۞
Muhammad is the Messenger of Allāh and those with him are stern against the disbelievers, merciful among themselves. You see them bowing and prostrating, (in prayer) seeking bounty from Allāh and (His) pleasure. Their mark is on their faces from the trace of prostration. That is their description in the Tawrāh.	29	مُحَمَّدٌ رَسُولُ اللَّهِ ۚ وَالَّذِينَ مَعَهُ أَشِدَّاءُ عَلَى الْكُفَّارِ رُحَمَاءُ بَيْنَهُمْ ۖ تَرَاهُمْ رُكَّعًا سُجَّدًا يَبْتَغُونَ فَضْلًا مِنَ اللَّهِ وَرِضْوَانًا ۖ سِيمَاهُمْ فِي وُجُوهِهِمْ مِنْ أَثَرِ السُّجُودِ ۚ ذَلِكَ مَثَلُهُمْ فِي التَّوْرَاةِ ۚ وَمَثَلُهُمْ فِي الْإِنْجِيلِ كَزَرْعٍ أَخْرَجَ شَطْأَهُ فَآزَرَهُ فَاسْتَغْلَظَ فَاسْتَوَى عَلَى

And their description in the Bible is as a plant which produces its offshoots and strengthens them so they grow firm and stand upon their stalks, delighting the sowers so that Allāh may enrage by them the disbelievers. Allāh has promised those who believe and do righteous deeds among them forgiveness and a great reward.	29	سُوقِهِۦ يُعۡجِبُ الزُّرَّاعَ لِيَغِيظَ بِهِمُ الۡكُفَّارَ وَعَدَ اللَّهُ الَّذِينَ ءَامَنُوا۟ وَعَمِلُوا۟ الصَّـٰلِحَـٰتِ مِنۡهُم مَّغۡفِرَةً وَأَجۡرًا عَظِيمًا ۞

Sūrah Index

Kanzul Bāri

Kanzul Bāri provides a detailed commentary of the Ahādeeth contained in Saheeh al-Bukhāri. The commentary includes Imām Bukhāri's ﷺ biography, the status of his book, spiritual advice, inspirational accounts along with academic discussions related to Fiqh, its application and differences of opinion. Moreover, it answers objections arising in one's mind about certain Ahādeeth. Inquisitive students of Hadeeth will find this commentary a very useful reference book in the final year of their Ālim course for gaining a deeper understanding of the science of Hadeeth. **UK RRP: £15.00**

How to Become a Friend of Allāh ﷺ

The friends of Allāh ﷺ have been described in detail in the Holy Qur'ān and Āhadeeth. This book endeavours its readers to help create a bond with Allāh ﷺ in attaining His friendship as He is the sole Creator of all material and immaterial things. It is only through Allāh's ﷺ friendship, an individual will achieve happiness in this life and the Hereafter, hence eliminate worries, sadness, depression, anxiety and misery of this world. **UK RRP:**

Gems & Jewels

This book contains a selection of articles which have been gathered for the benefit of the readers covering a variety of topics on various aspects of daily life. It offers precious advice and anecdotes that contain moral lessons. The advice captivates its readers and will extend the narrowness of their thoughts to deep reflection, wisdom and appreciation of the purpose of our existence. **UK RRP: £4.00**

End of Time

This book is a comprehensive explanation of the three Sūrahs of Juzz Amma; Sūrah Takweer, Sūrah Infitār and Sūrah Mutaffifeen. This book is a continuation from the previous book of the same author, 'Horrors of Judgement Day'. The three Sūrahs vividly sketch out the scene of the Day of Judgement and describe the state of both the inmates of Jannah and Jahannam. Mufti Saiful Islām Sāhib provides an easy but comprehensive commentary of the three Sūrahs facilitating its understanding for the readers whilst capturing the horrific scene of the ending of the world and the conditions of mankind on that horrific Day. **UK RRP: £5.00**

Golden Legacy of Spain

Andalus (modern day Spain), the long lost history, was once a country that produced many great calibre of Muslim scholars comprising of Mufassirūn, Muhaddithūn, Fuqahā, judges, scientists, philosophers, surgeons, to name but a few. The Muslims conquered Andalus in 711 AD and ruled over it for eight-hundred years. This was known as the era of Muslim glory. Many non-Muslim Europeans during that time travelled to Spain to study under Muslim scholars. The remanences of the Muslim rule in Spain are manifested through their universities, magnificent palaces and Masājid carved with Arabic writings, standing even until today. In this book, Shaykh Mufti Saiful Islām shares some of his valuable experiences he witnessed during his journey to Spain. **UK RRP: £3.00**

Ideal Youth

This book contains articles gathered from various social media avenues; magazines, emails, WhatsApp and telegram messages that provide useful tips of advice for those who have the zeal to learn and consider changing their negative habits and behavior and become better Muslims to set a positive trend for the next generation. **UK RRP:£4:00**

Ideal Teacher

This book contains abundance of precious advices for the Ulamā who are in the teaching profession. It serves to present Islamic ethical principles of teaching and to remind every teacher of their moral duties towards their students. This book will Inshā-Allāh prove to be beneficial for newly graduates and scholars wanting to utilize their knowledge through teaching. **UK RRP:£4:00**

Ideal Student

This book is a guide for all students of knowledge in achieving the excellent qualities of becoming an ideal student. It contains precious advices, anecdotes of our pious predecessors and tips in developing good morals as a student. Good morals is vital for seeking knowledge. A must for all students if they want to develop their Islamic Knowledge. **UK RRP:£4:00**

Ideal Parents

This book contains a wealth of knowledge in achieving the qualities of becoming ideal parents. It contains precious advices, anecdotes of our pious predecessors and tips in developing good parenthood skills. Good morals is vital for seeking knowledge. A must for all parents . **UK RRP:£4:00**

Ideal Couple

This book is a compilation of inspiring stories and articles containing useful tips and life skills for every couple. Marriage life is a big responsibility and success in marriage is only possible if the couple know what it means to be an ideal couple. **UK RRP:£4:00**

Ideal Role Model

This book is a compilation of sayings and accounts of our pious predecessors. The purpose of this book is so we can learn from our pious predecessors the purpose of this life and how to attain closer to the Creator. Those people who inspires us attaining closeness to our Creator are our true role models. A must everyone to read. **UK RRP:£4:00**

Bangladesh– A Land of Natural Beauty

This book is a compilation of our respected Shaykh's journeys to Bangladesh including visits to famous Madāris and Masājid around the country. The Shaykh shares some of his thought provoking experiences and his personal visits with great scholars in Bangladesh. **UK RRP: £4.00**

Pearls from the Qur'an

This series begins with the small Sūrahs from 30th Juzz initially, unravelling its heavenly gems, precious advices and anecdotes worthy of personal reflection. It will most definitely benefit both those new to as well as advanced students of the science of Tafsīr. The purpose is to make it easily accessible for the general public in understanding the meaning of the Holy Qur'ān. **UK RRP: £10.00**

The Lady who Spoke the Qur'ān

The Holy Prophet ﷺ was sent as a role model who was the physical form of the Holy Qur'ān. Following the ways of the Holy Prophet ﷺ in every second of our lives is pivotal for success. This booklet tells us the way to gain this success. It also includes an inspirational incident of an amazing lady who only spoke from the Holy Qur'an throughout her life. We will leave it to our readers to marvel at her intelligence, knowledge and piety expressed in this breath-taking episode. **UK RRP:£3:00**

Sleepers of the Cave

The Tafsīr of Sūrah Kahf is of crucial importance in this unique and challenging time we are currently living in. This book is evidently beneficial for all Muslims, more crucial for the general public. This is because Mufti Sāhib gives us extensive advice on how to act accordingly when treading the path of seeking knowledge. Readers will find amazing pieces of advice in terms of etiquettes regarding seeking knowledge and motivation, Inshā-Allāh. **UK RRP:£5:00**

When the Heavens Split

This book contains the commentary of four Sūrahs from Juzz Amma namely; Sūrah Inshiqāq, Sūrah Burūj, Sūrah Tāriq and Sūrah A'lā. The first two Sūrahs contain a common theme of capturing the scenes and events of the Last Day and how this world will come to an end. However, all four Sūrahs mentioned, have a connection of the journey of humanity, reflection on nature, how nature changes and most importantly, giving severe warnings to mankind about the punishments and exhorting them to prepare for the Hereafter through good deeds and refraining from sins. **UK RRP: £4.00**

Don't Delay Your Nikāh

Marriage plays an important role in our lives. It is a commemoration of the union of two strangers who will spend the rest of their remaining lives with one another. Marriage ought to transpire comfort and tranquillity whereby the couple share one another's sorrow and happiness. It is strongly recommended that our brothers and sisters read and benefit from this book and try to implement it into our daily lives in order to once more revive the Sunnah of the Holy Prophet ﷺ on such occasions and repel the prevalent sins and baseless customs.

UK RRP:£3:00

Miracle of the Holy Qur'ān

The scholars of Islām are trying to wake us all up, however, we are busy dreaming of the present world and have forgotten our real destination. Shaykh Mufti Saiful Islām Sāhib has been conducted Tafsīr of the Holy Qur'ān every week for almost two decades with the purpose of reviving its teachings and importance. This book is a transcription of two titles; Miracle of the Holy Qur'ān and The Revelation of the Holy Qur'ān, both delivered during the weekly Tafsīr sessions. **UK RRP:£3:00**

Dearest Act to Allāh
Today our Masājid have lofty structures, engraved brickworks, exquisite chandeliers and laid rugs, but they are spiritually deprived due to the reason that the Masājid are used for social purposes including backbiting and futile talk rather than the performance of Salāh, Qur'ān recitation and the spreading of true authentic Islamic knowledge. This book elaborates on the etiquettes of the Masjid and the importance of Salāh with Quranic and prophetic proofs along with some useful anecdotes to emphasize their importance. **UK RRP:£3:00**

Don't Delay Your Nikāh
Marriage plays an important role in our lives. It is a commemoration of the union of two strangers who will spend the rest of their remaining lives with one another. Marriage ought to transpire comfort and tranquillity whereby the couple share one another's sorrow and happiness. It is strongly recommended that our brothers and sisters read and benefit from this book and try to implement it into our daily lives in order to once more revive the Sunnah of the Holy Prophet ﷺ on such occasions and repel the prevalent sins and baseless customs.

UK RRP:£3:00

Miracle of the Holy Qur'ān
The scholars of Islām are trying to wake us all up, however, we are busy dreaming of the present world and have forgotten our real destination. Shaykh Mufti Saiful Islām Sāhib has been conducted Tafsīr of the Holy Qur'ān every week for almost two decades with the purpose of reviving its teachings and importance. This book is a transcription of two titles; Miracle of the Holy Qur'ān and The Revelation of the Holy Qur'ān, both delivered during the weekly Tafsīr sessions. **UK RRP:£3:00**

You are what you Eat
Eating Halāl and earning a lawful income plays a vital role in the acceptance of all our Ibādāt (worship) and good deeds. Mufti Saiful Islām Sāhib has presented a discourse on this matter in one of his talks. I found the discourse to be very beneficial, informative and enlightening on the subject of Halāl and Harām that clarifies its importance and status in Islām. I strongly recommend my Muslim brothers and sisters to read this treatise and to study it thoroughly.

UK RRP:£3:00

Protection from Black Magic

These last ten Sūrahs are not only distinct in their meanings and message which will be discussed in this book, but also the fact that every Muslim should have these Sūrahs committed to memory as a minimum requirement in seeking refuge in Allāh ﷻ from all harm and evil, and every imperfection as well as seeking solace and peace in understanding His might and attributes. **UK RRP:£5:00**

Nurturing Children in Islam

Bringing up children has never been an easy duty. The challenges do not get easier as they get older either. Our emotions and other priorities sometimes hinder in nurturing our children, and as such, we fail to assist our children in reaching their potential by continually stumbling over our own perception of what we consider as ideal children. Our duty to our children is not without accountability. Our neglect and lack of interest in our children will be held to task. **UK RRP:£5:00**

Contemporary Fiqh

This book is a selection of detailed *Fiqhi* (juridical) articles on contemporary legal issues. These detailed articles provide an in depth and elaborative response to some of the queries posted to us in our Fatawa department over the last decade. The topics discussed range between purity, domestic issues, Halāl and Harām, Islamic medical ethics, marital issues, rituals and so forth. Many of the juristic cases are unprecedented as a result of the ongoing societal changes and newly arising issues. **UK RRP:£6:00**

Ideal Society

In this book, 'Ideal Society' which is a commentary of Sūrah Hujurāt, Shaykh Mufti Saiful Islām Sāhib explains the lofty status of our beloved Prophet ﷺ, the duties of the believers and general mankind and how to live a harmonious social life, which is free from evil, jealousy and vices. Inshā-Allāh, this book will enable and encourage the readers to adopt a social life which will ultimately bring happiness and joy to each and every individual.

UK RRP:£5:00

Best of Stories

Sūrah Yūsuf is more than just a story of one of our beloved Prophets ﷺ, there is much wisdom and lessons to be learnt and understood. All the knowledge comes from our honourable Shaykh, inspiration and Ustādh, Shaykh Mufti Saiful Islām Sāhib. May Allāh ﷻ shower Mufti Sāhib with mercy and accept the day in, day out effort he carries out in the work of Dīn. **UK RRP:£4:00**

Call of Nuh

For 950 years, Sayyidunā Nūh ﷺ persevered night and day in continuous succession in preaching the message; unwavering and relentless in his mission. Not once did he feel that his calling was in vain. He stood firm and resolute in continuing with the mission that he was sent with, in proclaiming the message of the oneness of Allāh ﷻ; year after year, decade upon decade, century after century, but this failed to convince the people of the truth. **UK RRP:£4:00**

Quranic Wonders

The science of Tafsīr in itself is very vast, hence the compilation of these specific verses provides the reader with a simple and brief commentary. It is aimed to equip the reader with a small glimpse of the profound beauty of the Holy Qur'ān so that they can gain the passion to study further in depth. It is hoped that this will become a means of encouragement to increase the zeal and enthusiasm to recite and inculcate the teachings of the Holy Qur'ān into our daily lives. **UK RRP:£5:00**

Contentment of the Heart

The purification of the soul and its rectification are matters of vital importance which were brought by our Holy Prophet e to this Ummah. The literal meaning of Tazkiyah is 'to cleanse'. The genuine Sūfis assert that the foundation and core of all virtuous character is sincerity and the basis for all evil characteristics and traits is love for this world. This book endeavors to address certain spiritual maladies and how to overcome them using Islamic principles. **UK RRP:£5:00**

163